PUSHING THE LIMITS

AMERICAN WOMEN
1940-1961

PUSHING THE LIMITS

AMERICAN WOMEN
1940-1961

Elaine Tyler May

OXFORD UNIVERSITY PRESS

New York • Oxford

For Sarah Lillian May
Keep pushing the limits!

Oxford University Press

Oxford New York Toronto
Delhi Bombay Calcutta Madras Karachi
Kuala Lumpur Singapore Hong Kong Tokyo
Nairobi Dar es Salaam Cape Town
Melbourne Auckland Madrid

and associated companies in
Berlin Ibadan

Copyright © 1994 by Elaine Tyler May

Published by Oxford University Press, Inc., 200 Madison Avenue, New York, New York 10016

Oxford is a registered trademark of Oxford University Press

Library of Congress Cataloging-in-Publication Data

May, Elaine Tyler.
Pushing the limits : American women, 1940-1961 / Elaine Tyler May.
p. cm. — (Young Oxford history of women in the United States : v.9)
Includes bibliographical references and index
Summary: Discusses the role of women during World War II and in the postwar years of both expanding and contracting opportunities
for them, as many sought their rightful place as full American citizens.
ISBN 0-19-508084-X
1. Women—United States—History—20th century—Juvenile literature. 2. United States—Social conditions—1945—Juvenile
literature. 3. United States—Social conditions—1945—Juvenile literature. [1. Women—History—20th century. 2. Women—Social
conditions. 3. United States—Social conditions—1933-1945. 4. United States—Social conditions—1945-]
I. Title. II. Series.
HQ1420.M374   1994
305.4'0973—dc20   93-16161
CIP
AC

3 5 7 9 8 6 4 2
Printed in the United States of America
on acid-free paper

Design: Leonard Levitsky
Picture research: Lisa Kirchner, Laura Kreiss

On the cover: "Calship Burner" by Edna Reindel, 1943.
Frontispiece: Women install fixtures in the fuselage of a B-17 bomber at the Douglas Aircraft plant, October 1942.

CONTENTS

INTRODUCTION

Americans living in the middle of the 20th century saw momentous change. A decade of severe economic depression in the 1930s was followed by the largest-scale war the world had ever seen. The Allies' defeat of Germany and Japan in World War II brought formal peace and new prosperity but also the beginning of a tense and long-lasting cold war between the United States and the Soviet Union.

Women's lives in the United States reflected and helped to shape these world changes. As workers, mothers, citizens, artists, consumers, and community leaders, women participated in the making of an American way of life and the rise of the United States to global power in the mid-20th century. Just how crucial women's contributions to the nation were became obvious during the world war, when war production demands drew women (especially married women) into manufacturing jobs, and broadcast the image of Rosie the Riveter. In the postwar years, the historical parts that women played were perhaps even more prominent. This can be seen in the Baby Boom, the migration to the suburbs, the ballooning of white-collar jobs, and the reliance on consumerism as the engine of economic expansion, as well as in the civil rights and peace movements and in artistic innovation. In dramatic incidents and individualized detail, this book shows the variety and importance of American women's

Chicago's Union Station was the scene of many a fond farewell as servicemen went off to war.

experiences during the war and postwar decades, demonstrating that the history of the period cannot be fully understood without focusing on changes in women's lives.

This book is part of a series that covers the history of women in the United States from the 17th through 20th century. Traditional historical writing has dealt almost entirely with men's lives because men have, until very recently, been the heads of state, the political officials, judges, ministers, and business leaders who have wielded the most visible and recorded power. But for several recent decades, new interest has arisen in social and cultural history, where common people are the actors who create trends and mark change as well as continuity. An outpouring of research and writing on women's history has been part of this trend to look at individuals and groups who have not held the reins of rule in their own hands but nonetheless participated in making history. The motive to address and correct sexual inequality in society has also vitally influenced women's history, on the thinking that knowledge of the past is essential to creating justice for the future.

A World War II veteran enjoys his young family as he studies for a civilian career.

The histories in this series look at many aspects of women's lives. The books ask new questions about the course of American history. How did the type and size of families change, and what difference did that make in people's lives? What expectations for women differed from those for men, and how did such expectations change over the centuries? What roles did women play in the economy? What form did women's political participation take when they could not vote? And how did politics change when women did gain full citizenship? How did women work with other women who were like or unlike them, as well as with men, for social and political goals? What sex-specific constraints or opportunities did they face? The series aims to understand the diverse women who have peopled American history by investigating their work and leisure, family patterns, political activities, forms of organization, and outstanding accomplishments. Standard events of American history, from the settling of the continent to the American revolution, the Civil War, industrialization, American entry onto the world stage, and world wars, are all here, too, but seen from the point of view of women's experiences. Together, the answers to new questions and the treatment of old ones from women's points of view make up a compelling narrative of four centuries of history in the United States.

—Nancy F. Cott

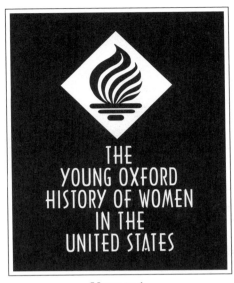

THE YOUNG OXFORD HISTORY OF WOMEN IN THE UNITED STATES

VOLUME 1
The Tried and the True
Native American Women Confronting Colonization

VOLUME 2
The Colonial Mosaic
American Women 1600-1760

VOLUME 3
The Limits of Independence
American Women 1760-1800

VOLUME 4
Breaking New Ground
American Women 1800-1848

VOLUME 5
An Unfinished Battle
American Women 1848-1865

VOLUME 6
Laborers for Liberty
American Women 1865-1890

VOLUME 7
New Paths to Power
American Women 1890-1910

VOLUME 8
From Ballots to Breadlines
American Women 1920-1940

VOLUME 9
Pushing the Limits
American Women 1940-1961

VOLUME 10
The Road to Equality
American Women Since 1962

CHAPTER 1

PRELUDE TO
WAR AND COLD WAR

In the years before World War II, during the Great Depression of the 1930s, Luisa Moreno came to the United States from Guatemala. Although she came from a wealthy family, she found herself working long hours at a sewing machine in a New York City sweatshop, struggling to support her unemployed husband, an artist from Mexico, and their baby. When World War II broke out, she moved to California and worked in a canning factory, where she urged Mexicana workers (women whose families came from Mexico) to join a union and fight for better wages and working conditions. By the late 1940s, she had become a major union leader. Ultimately, her union was demolished, a victim of the anti-Communist hysteria of the postwar era.

During the war, while Luisa Moreno was moving from East to West to begin organizing women workers, Margaret Starks was moving from the South to the West. The daughter of African-American tenant farmers, Starks joined the huge migration of blacks who moved out of the South during World War II in search of better jobs. Margaret Starks moved to Richmond, California, a booming war-industry town, where she ran a blues club, edited a black newspaper, and became active in the National Association for the Advancement of Colored People (NAACP), an organization that would help to fuel the emerging civil rights movement.

A North Dakota family exhibits the ravages of the depression. Short of coal and bedding, with the father injured, the mother had to deliver all of her own children.

Under the stern gaze of their supervisor, women at a California cannery pit and process peaches.

While Luisa Moreno and Margaret Starks were beginning their lives as activists, Betty Goldstein, a young college-educated Jew, moved to New York's Greenwich Village, where she spent the war years working as a journalist and participating in left-wing politics. After the war, having given up a fellowship to pursue a Ph.D., she followed the advice given to most white women at the time: She married, moved to the suburbs, and became a full-time wife and mother. She dedicated herself to homemaking until the early 1960s, when she wrote a stinging criticism of the frustrating life of a housewife and urged other women like herself to leave their kitchens and pursue careers. Her book would help to galvanize thousands of middle-class housewives into the new feminist movement.

These three women are among many whose lives will unfold in the chapters ahead. They had very different experiences during the 1940s and 1950s. But they were all profoundly affected by the Great Depression, World War II, and the Cold War that followed. Wartime opened up new possibilities for all three women, and the postwar years of the Cold War presented them with new obstacles. The story of American women during these years is one of expanding and contracting opportunities.

These decades were tumultuous for all Americans. When the Japanese attacked the United States at Pearl Harbor in 1941, the country went to war, fighting Nazi aggression and genocide in Europe and Japanese expansion in Asia. Peace came in 1945, but it was a tense and fragile peace marked by what was called the Cold War between the two new superpowers, the United States and the Soviet Union. The Cold War, or period of mutual hostility between the superpowers, lasted until the late 1980s.

Betty Friedan, future feminist author, and her husband, Carl, supervise a children's birthday party in their suburban home during the 1950s.

When the United States entered World War II, the worst economic depression in the nation's history ended suddenly, followed by decades of prosperity with a booming economy. These were the years of the major demographic upheaval of the century: the Baby Boom. Marriage rates increased, men and women married younger, the divorce rate declined, the birth rate soared, and Americans streamed into rapidly expanding suburbs. Technological advances came rapidly: the United States dropped the first nuclear weapons on Hiroshima and Nagasaki at the end of World War II, unleashing the atomic age; television came to American homes in 1950; houses filled with appliances.

Mainstream politics dwindled to a call for unity and patriotism in defense of war and Cold War aims. But beneath the surface, artists, activists, and those excluded from the bland political mood of the Cold War consensus planted the seeds of massive social change. The civil rights movement took shape in the South and began the agitation that would transform race relations more profoundly than anything since the Civil War. It also laid the groundwork for other movements that would emerge later on behalf of women, farm workers, American Indians, gays and lesbians, and other groups seeking their rightful place as full American citizens.

American women were part of all these dramatic events and developments. They shaped them and were also affected by them. Some women had more choices than others, but they all took advantage of new opportunities and pushed against the constraints that remained. They were not watching from the sidelines; they were on the march. But often their choices were limited. These were not years of steady progress. Opportunities opened in some areas for some women, and shrank or closed for others. As a result, women developed creative strategies for their lives and sought to transform the institutions in which they lived and worked.

During these mid-century decades, individual opportunities were determined largely according to gender and race. In other words, if two individuals had the same resources in terms of money and education, and one was female and the other male, those two individuals would have had very different life choices to make. If they were both employed, the man's job would probably require more skill and responsibility, and hold more opportunities for advancement. Even if the man and the woman held exactly the same job, his pay would be higher. But it would be much more likely that the woman would not hold a job at all.

If the two individuals were both women, but one was black and one was white, they, too, would face very different options. Let us consider a white woman who we will call Jane, and a black woman we will call Bertha. If Jane and Bertha both entered college after the war, Jane would probably have married and dropped out of college

An Ohio steelworker and his family in a typical postwar housing project. In return for scarce housing, the original residents pledged 3,000 hours of labor apiece to help build additional units.

to become a full-time homemaker, while Bertha would have been much more likely to graduate and pursue employment. If Jane happened to get pregnant before she was married, she would probably have been persuaded to give up her baby for adoption or marry the baby's father immediately. If the same thing happened to Bertha, she would have been encouraged to keep her baby, and might marry the baby's father at some future time.

If Bertha and Jane both married, they would most likely marry World War II veterans and begin to have babies right away. If both of their husbands had steady work with a modest but stable income, Jane and her husband would undoubtedly have purchased a new home in the suburbs, paid a small monthly mortgage, and turned their energies toward private life with their family. Bertha and her husband would have been excluded from that suburban neighborhood because they were black, even if they could afford to purchase the home. They would probably have remained in the city, where they would have paid more for apartment rent than Jane and her husband would have spent on their house mortgage. Bertha would have been more likely than Jane to hold a job outside the home to help make ends meet. But if Jane decided to take a job, she would probably have earned more than Bertha, even though Bertha had a college degree. Neither woman, however, would have earned as much as her husband. Jane would probably have shunned politics, unless she became involved in her local League of Women Voters, working on behalf of good government, or the PTA. Bertha, however, might have joined her friends and neighbors in the local NAACP, and worked for racial equality.

These two women, with similar incomes, faced dramatically different possibilities in their lives because of their race. But race did not always function in predictable ways. Why would Bertha be more likely to graduate from college? Why would she be more likely to become politically active than Jane? Why would they face such different consequences for their premarital sexual activity? These differences reveal some of the invisible barriers that American women faced as they pushed the limits of postwar life.

Although there had already been decades of effort on behalf of the rights of women and people of color, equal opportunity was a long way off. In some ways, the postwar years actually represented

In contrast to suburban comfort, many blacks in Northern cities endured shabby conditions, as in this Philadelphia slum apartment.

backward steps on the path toward full equality. These were decades when racial and gender divisions became rigid, even though class divisions—especially between the prosperous working class and the comfortable middle class—softened.

The first major opportunity for women to expand their opportunities came with World War II. Most of the changes involving American women in the early 1940s resulted from the wartime emergency. Emergency was nothing new to the young women and men coming of age at the time. They had been reared on the trials and hardships of the Great Depression. The depression of the 1930s, like the war that brought it to an end, disrupted the expected roles and responsibilities of women and men. But the depression, like the war, was a temporary crisis calling for a short-term emergency response, and for that reason the potential for long-term full equality was never realized.

During the depression, women struggled to survive and set their sights on a brighter future. Mrs. Szymanski, a Polish-American woman, recalled how life at home was disrupted:

> We both worked before the Depression, and we bought a home and went into debt. When the depression broke out ... it's unbelievable how hard those years were, because today I can't believe how we lived through it. I lost my job and papa lost his job. Papa didn't work a whole year and I, about half a year. We had little

Viola and Broniu then. I had to be away from them, running around for work. There were two hundred, three hundred people around one factory, looking for work. Maybe one person would be hired where some place was running a bit, but almost every place was closed. People wandered around those factory walls looking for work all day, day after day. There was no help.... I don't know how we lived. We went into debt up to our ears ... and then when things started to get better, well we paid off our debts, where it was most urgent.

After losing her factory job, Mrs. Szymanski worked full-time at home making clothes. But she still had her other household responsibilities.

I had to cut the fabric and had to make the suit all by myself and finished to give to the customer. That's taking a lot of time, and each suit has to be different. I liked it, but I had to take care of my family.... I didn't have time to clean my house or cook; my husband would come from his work hungry, tired, and my daughter was still at school.... We are just about to sit and eat and somebody [a customer] is at the door or calls.... I worked like this for three years, so I almost had a nervous breakdown, and the doctor told me that either you close it up or you are going to get sick, seriously sick.

Mrs. Szymanski would be extremely relieved when the depression ended and life could ease up somewhat. She and her family suffered from the economic strain. Her daughter undoubtedly viewed her mother's exhausting days with alarm. Many daughters during the depression saw how hard their parents worked. Men struggled to earn enough to provide for their families; women tried to be good homemakers. As one immigrant daughter later recalled,

[T]he emigrant mother often had to work not only in her home, but outside as well, under the most harrowing conditions.... For the son, it was important and necessary to obtain an education, so he could escape the sweatshop of his father. For the daughter, however, the most precious legacy was an escape from the hard work and drudgery of her mother and the attainment of leisure— the very leisure this emigrant mother never knew herself, and which she so desperately needed.... To this emigrant mother, education was only necessary for her son to get a better job, and the daughter, with nothing else besides her femininity, would, with luck, marry well and thereby achieve the leisure her mother never knew.

These dreams for a better life—a good job for the man, a life as

Canning skills learned during the depression helped resourceful American women feed their families despite wartime shortages of sugar, butter, and other commodities.

homemaker for the woman—were the goals of many depression-weary Americans. In these dreams lay the seeds of the postwar era, when men would try to provide for their families in ways that were so difficult for their fathers during the depression, and women would finally have the luxury to stay home with their children. But there were other legacies of the depression. The 1930s was a time not only of economic hardship and misery, but of tremendous energy and radicalism. Many believed that fundamental flaws in the American economic and political system were responsible for the crisis, and that the only cure would be a complete overhaul of the system. Those reform-minded citizens believed that recovery would be achieved not simply by returning to the ways of the past, but by changing the system.

Because of widespread human suffering, the federal government began to intervene in private life to an unprecedented extent. President Franklin Roosevelt's program for economic recovery, the New Deal, provided jobs and relief, and Americans began to have hope that the crisis would end, even though the depression lingered, unresolved, throughout the 1930s. The New Deal helped to create a spirit of optimism and a willingness for change that permeated the nation.

The New Deal did a great deal to ease the suffering of many during the depression, but it did nothing to eradicate poverty or solve the economic crisis. As late as 1941, 40 percent of all American families lived below the poverty level, and almost 8 million workers earned less than the legal minimum wage. The depression did not affect everyone in the same way, but it created a general state of crisis that altered daily life for millions of women and men.

One role that changed was the place of marriage in people's lives. The marriage rate had plummeted to an all-time low during the early 1930s, from nearly 90 per 1,000 unmarried women in 1920 to just over 60 a decade later. Men were reluctant to marry if they thought they would not be able to provide for a family. The birthrate also declined in the 1930s, and divorces increased as families collapsed under financial strain.

Many young single women took jobs to help support their parents and siblings. Employment offered an alternative to young marriage and economic dependence. One young woman was in no hurry to marry: "It's not that I didn't want to get married, but when you are working and have your own money…" she did not feel compelled. Many others of her generation made similar decisions. One explained, "During all the years I worked, I had a boyfriend, but we both had responsibilities at home…. Now they say 'career woman' but at the time you wouldn't call yourself that. It's just because you felt you had a responsibility at home, too."

These women felt a sense of obligation to their parents, but they also took pride in their economic contributions. In spite of the discrimination women faced in the paid labor force, many achieved some measure of independence they were not so eager to give up to become dependent in someone else's home—especially with men's employment as precarious as it was. As a result, more than 6 million single women in the 1930s were making it on their own and contributing to the support of their parents' households.

A Texas woman sews mattress ticking as part of the cotton mattress demonstration program, one of many New Deal projects to provide employment and economic recovery.

The popular culture at the time, particularly movies and fan magazines, glamorized single working women and affirmed their active role in public life. Radio soap operas featured independent career women such as "Dr. Kate," "Hilda Hope, M.D.," and "Her Honor, Nancy James." Some of these programs continued into the war years, such as "Joyce Jordan, Girl Intern," which became "Joyce Jordan, M.D." four years later in 1942. "Ma Perkins," operator of a lumber yard, began in 1933 and lasted 27 years.

Movies featured similar heroines. In *His Girl Friday*, a popular film of 1940 starring Rosalind Russell, the feisty reporter has just divorced her work-obsessed boss (played by Cary Grant). She proves her grit by rescuing a hapless criminal and outwitting all of her male colleagues. Even though she agrees to marry again at the end of the movie, she has established herself as a smart and tough professional who can do a "man's job." It is not at all clear, however, that she will settle down into marital bliss. Similarly, Scarlett O'Hara, the shrewd heroine of the popular novel and film *Gone With the Wind*, survives hard times through her intelligence and determination. But in the end her marriage is in shambles. Hollywood encouraged the independence of women and the equality of the sexes. But it failed to portray families that included independent women. Rather, these tough and rugged heroines were admired as *women*, not as wives.

These ideas prevailed in the world beyond Hollywood as well. Even the most radical measures of the New Deal, created to ease

Rosalind Russell, as a spunky reporter, starred opposite Cary Grant in the 1940 film His Girl Friday. *Many prewar films featured strong, competent career women.*

hardship, failed to promote the possibility of a new family structure based on gender equality. Although female unemployment was a severe problem, and many families depended on the earnings of both spouses, federal policies supported unemployed male breadwinners but discouraged married women from seeking jobs. Section 213 of the Economy Act of 1932 mandated that whenever personnel reductions took place in the executive branch, a married person would be the first discharged if his or her spouse was also a government employee. As a result, 1,600 married women were dismissed from their federal jobs. Many state and local governments followed suit; three out of four cities excluded married women from teaching, and eight states passed laws excluding them from state jobs. The government provided relief for families in need, but not jobs for married women.

The New Deal also failed to remedy wage inequities. Men still earned much more than women, even if they held similar jobs. By ignoring the plight of working women, the government actually contributed to the deterioration of their economic status. It would provide unemployment or even take over as breadwinner for an unemployed head of household, but it would not provide well-paying jobs for women, day care facilities for their children, or any other measures that would help reduce women's economic dependence on men.

Yet men had a difficult time providing for their families. Unemployment placed severe strains on marriage. Going on relief may have helped the family budget, but it would do little for the breadwinner's feelings of failure. Frequently, wives and mothers who had never been employed took jobs to provide support for their families. Their employment often meant facing social condemnation as well as miserably low wages. Working wives faced intense pressure to give up their jobs even if their families depended on their earnings. Although women rarely displaced male workers—the vast majority held "women's jobs" that men would not take in any case—they were considered selfish if they were employed when men were out of work. A 1936 Gallup poll indicated that 82 percent of those surveyed (including three fourths of the women) believed that wives of employed husbands should not work outside the home. By 1939, nearly 90 percent of the men who were polled believed that "women should not hold a job after marriage," and most women still agreed. Public praise was reserved for self-supporting single women, or for frugal and resourceful homemakers who helped their families through the crisis.

The depression opened the way for a new type of family with shared breadwinning, and an economy based on equality of the sexes. But it also created the wish for a time when fathers alone could provide a decent living, and mothers were freed from outside employment. In the end, that wish for separate roles for women and men won out over the potential for equality. If the paid labor force had been a more hospitable place, and if public policies had fostered equal opportunities for women, young people in the 1930s might have been less inclined to set their sights on becoming breadwinner-husbands and homemaker-wives. Realistic long-term job prospects for women might have prompted new ways of structuring the family and the economy. In the face of persistent obstacles, however, that potential withered. But when World War II brought a sudden end to the depression, bringing full employment and a booming economy, many of these obstacles would be removed.

CHAPTER 2

WORLD WAR II:
THE CHANCE FOR CHANGE

Worldorld War II ushered in sudden, dramatic changes for American women. One young woman recalled the breathless excitement of life in Chicago during wartime:

Chicago was just humming, no matter where I went. The bars were jammed, and unless you were an absolute dog, you could pick up anyone you wanted to.... There were servicemen of all varieties roaming the streets all the time. There was never, never a shortage of young, healthy bucks.... We never thought of getting tired. Two, three hours of sleep was normal.... I'd go down to the office every morning half dead, but with a smile on my face, and report in for work. There was another girl there who was having a ball too, and we took turns going into the back room and taking a nap on the floor behind a desk.

Work changed too. When the men left to fight the war, women took jobs that had never been available to them in the past, because men had always done those jobs. But now that the men were gone, somebody had to do them, and women showed themselves to be capable of all kinds of work. Almira Bondelid recalls what happened when her husband left for overseas: "I decided to stay in San Diego and went to work in a dime store. That was a terrible place to work, and as soon as I could I got a job at Convair [an aircraft manufacturer].... I worked in the tool department as a draftsman, and by

Women defense workers wearing protective hair nets polish the noses of Air Force bombers in the Long Beach, California, factory of Douglas Aircraft.

"Rosie the Riveter" had many roles: doing metalwork at the Marinship Corp. (top left), cleaning blast furnaces at a U.S. Steel factory (bottom), and preparing machine screws to be dipped in a protective coating (top right).

the time I left there two years later I was designing long drill jigs for parts of the wing and hull of B-24s."

With these new opportunities for work and play, women during the war glimpsed the possibility for long-term changes that might have led to full equality for women. But that potential was never fully realized. Wartime needs caused a temporary crisis, and women's new activities were expected to last only "for the duration." Some of the changes turned out to be much more lasting. But the upheavals that brought sexual adventure to the single woman in Chicago and exciting new work to the wife in San Diego ended after the war.

When war broke out, women rapidly entered jobs in war-related industries. Many of these women had been employed before the war, mostly in low-paying, nonunion jobs in laundries, department stores, restaurants, and hotels, where they earned an average of $24.50 a week, compared to $40.35 a week for wartime manufacturing jobs. During the war, 300,000 women worked in the aircraft industry alone. Many assembled B-29 bombers, the mainstay of the U.S. Air Force. Others—welders, draftswomen, and machinists—built tanks and warships and made ammunition. Women also worked in nondefense industries such as machine shops, steel mills, oil refineries, railroad roundhouses, and lumber mills, as replacements for the men who had gone overseas. In all, women comprised half of this work force. The Office of War Information noted that war production work had "disproved the old bugaboo that women have no mechanical ability and that they are a distracting influence in industry."

Nevertheless, the nation remained uneasy about these new work roles for women. As large numbers of married women took jobs for the first time, many observers expressed alarm. *Fortune* magazine reported, "There are practically no unmarried women left to draw upon.... This leaves, as the next potential source of industrial workers, the housewives.... We are a kindly, somewhat sentimental people with strong, ingrained ideas about what women should or should not do. Many thoughtful citizens are seriously disturbed over the wisdom of bringing married women into the factories."

With war following on the heels of the depression, traditional domestic roles were once again thrown into disarray. But it was not until 1943 that government and industry began to recruit women actively. Eventually, the stigma attached to employment for married women evaporated, and women were urged to work as a patriotic duty, in order to keep the war economy booming while the men went off to fight.

As women rushed eagerly to take challenging and well-paying defense jobs, recruiters did their best to claim that the work would not diminish their femininity. "Rosie the Riveter," a young woman in overalls working to build ships and planes, became a national symbol; pictures of attractive "Rosies" graced magazine covers and posters. Marilyn Monroe first gained attention when her photograph appeared in *Yank,* a magazine for servicemen. She was pictured not as the Hollywood sex goddess she would later become, but as a typical Rosie the Riveter, in overalls at her job in a defense plant.

Employers and recruiters insisted that women's new jobs merely extended their domestic skills. Boeing Aircraft boasted of "pretty girls in smart slack outfits showing how easy it is to work on a wiring board." The propaganda film *Glamour Girls of '43* compared industrial work to domestic crafts: "Instead of cutting the lines of a dress, this woman cuts the pattern of aircraft parts. Instead of baking a cake, this woman is cooking gears to reduce the tension in the gears after use.... After a short apprenticeship, this

This poster issued by the government's War Production Board saluted the contributions of women who kept the country's factories going during the war.

woman can operate a drill press just as easily as a juice extractor in her own kitchen." *Fortune* magazine described a woman operating a steel-cutting machine as if she were making a dress: "Tailor-made suit cut to Axis size! . . . Skillful Van Dorn seamstress, with scissors of oxyacetylene, cloth of bullet-proof steel, and pattern shaped to our enemy's downfall!" These women would remain glamorous, as one advertisement for cleaning noted in verse:

> Oh, aren't we cute and snappy
> in our cover-alls and slacks?
> And since the tags say 'Sanforized'
> we'll stay as cute as tacks!"

Women faced constant reminders that they were different from the male workers they replaced. Even when viewed in the most positive light, their work appeared as a temporary interruption of their

Women defense workers in California adapt their domestic skills to sewing parachutes.

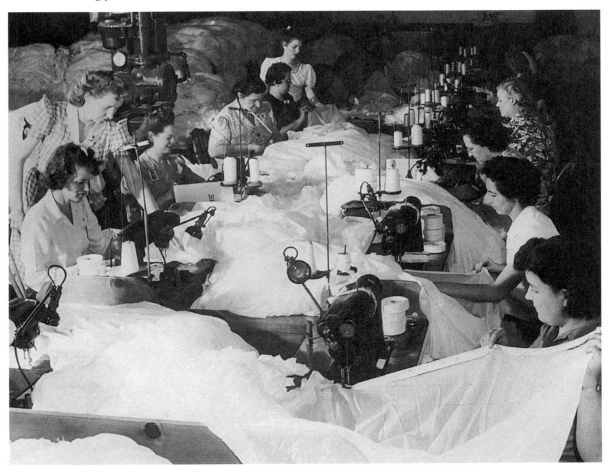

feminine routine. As *Life* magazine noted in an article on "Girl Pilots," "Girls are very serious about their chance to fly for the Army at Avenger Field, even when it means giving up nail polish, beauty parlors, and dates for a regimented 22½ weeks.... They each have on the G.I. coveralls, called zoot suits in Avenger Field lingo, that are regulation uniform for all working hours. Though suits are not very glamorous, the girls like their comfort and freedom."

Dressed like men and doing traditional "men's work," these women were not treated like men. They earned less than men earned for the same work, and they often faced unwanted male attention. One female war worker complained,

A corps of women replaced men as drivers at the U.S. Army quartermaster depot in San Antonio, Texas. Their uniforms consisted of blue slacks, coat, overseas cap, white shirts, brown or blue socks, and oxford shoes.

> At times it gets to be a pain in the neck when the man who is supposed to show you work stops showing it to you because you have nicely but firmly asked him to keep his hands on his own knees; or when you have refused a date with someone and ever since then he has done everything in his power to make your work more difficult.... Somehow we'll have to make them understand that we are not very much interested in their strapping virility. That the display of their physique and the lure of their prowess leaves us cold. That although they have certainly convinced us that they are men and we are women, we'd really rather get on with our work.

In spite of the harassment, teasing, and unwanted sexual advances women war workers faced, they enjoyed their new jobs, and most wanted to keep them after the war. Unlike the depression, the war emergency opened the way for a new labor force that would no longer be divided into "men's jobs" and "women's jobs," but would instead bring men and women into the same jobs, working side by side. In addition, because so many men went into the armed forces, and so many women went to work, young Americans might have postponed marriage and childbearing, just as they had in the depression. But that did not happen. Instead, ironically, wartime encouraged family formation. The return of prosperity made it easier for young men and women to marry and have children.

Young married women, those most likely to have children at home, made the smallest gains in the labor force. Young mothers were encouraged to stay home. Although the Federal Works Agency invested nearly $50 million in day care centers to accommodate employed mothers during the war, such centers were generally con-

During the war, the federal government encouraged young mothers to stay home and care for their children. Often, the government helped build housing for these new families.

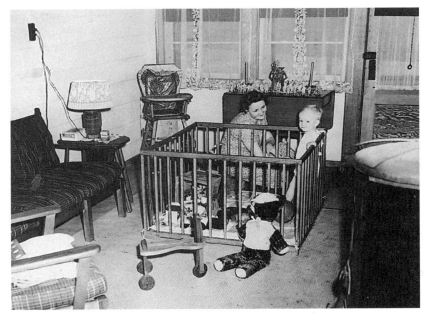

sidered harmful to a child's development. In all, only three thousand day care centers were established by the federal government, and even these were not filled to capacity.

Older married women who did not have young children at home were the fastest growing group in the paid labor force. By the end of the war fully 25 percent of all married women were employed—a huge gain from 15 percent at the end of the 1930s. But they worked for low wages. In 1939, the median annual income for women was $568, compared to $962 for men—and for black women it was a mere $246. By 1940 women comprised less than 10 percent of union members, although they were 25 percent of the workers.

Because women were still clustered in lower-skilled, lower-paying jobs, they had few bargaining levers to use to improve their working conditions. Relatively few held jobs like Rosie the Riveter. Most held the kinds of jobs women had always been able to get. If they worked in factories, their jobs were the lowest skilled and lowest paid. If they worked in white-collar jobs, they were most likely to be secretaries, clerks, and saleswomen. Or they worked in "pink-collar" service occupations such as waitressing or hairdressing. In spite of these limitations, women took advantage of wartime opportunities to earn better wages and enter new occupations. Even for women of color, who were usually given the least desirable and most menial jobs, often as cleaning women or chambermaids, the war offered the possibility of improved conditions.

American Indian women, for example, found new opportunities for work as well as political activism. World War II had a profound and lasting effect on the lives of American Indians. As men left the reservations to join the armed services or to take jobs in the cities, women moved into areas of activity that had previously been closed to them. Along with male enlistees, eight hundred Native American women joined the armed forces. Hundreds of others went to work in West Coast aircraft industries, where they worked along with white women as riveters, inspectors, and machinists. Approximately twelve thousand Indian women left the reservations for war-related work.

At the same time, Native American women assumed new leadership positions on as well as off the reservations. Many became teachers in Indian schools, while others took over farming chores that in some tribal communities had become men's work in the prewar years. In Wisconsin, Indian women began working in the lumber mills on the Menominee reservation for the first time. In many communities, the war loosened traditional work roles for men and women. Several Navajo women, for example, mastered tradition-

Menominee women working for the tribal lumber industry clear diseased plants from timberlands (left); a Zuni woman crafts fine silver jewelry (above).

ally male crafts such as silversmithing. Many Indian women as well as men went back and forth from cities to reservations during the war, establishing ties to urban communities that would grow after the war.

Wartime also broke down traditional tribal boundaries for many Indians, and opened up new possibilities for members of different tribes to meet and organize. The National Congress of American Indians (NCAI) was founded in 1944 to work on behalf of Indian people of all tribes, and women were central participants. Ruth Muskrat Bronson, an Oklahoma Cherokee and Mount Holyoke College graduate, became volunteer executive secretary and opened an office in Washington D.C., where she embarked on an energetic public relations campaign. A year later, at the second national convention of the NCAI, the delegates adopted a policy to elect at least one woman to the executive council each year. The war sparked a new militancy among American Indian activists. As Robert Yellowtail, a member of the NCAI council, wrote after the war, "What did 30,000 Indian soldiers fight for in the recent war? Surely it was for liberty and freedom of the American kind."

Those words resonated among African Americans as well, many of whom fought courageously in the war. The fight against fascism abroad brought home painfully the need to overcome racism at home. Membership in the National Association for the Advancement of Colored People (NAACP) rose dramatically during the war, and the Congress of Racial Equality (CORE) was founded in 1943. Although it would be another decade before the civil rights movement captured the attention of the entire nation, the struggle for racial equality continued throughout the war. Foreshadowing the courageous acts of civil disobedience that would later become the hallmark of the movement, during the war a black army nurse in Alabama brazenly boarded a bus in front of white passengers, and was beaten and jailed as a result.

African Americans joined the armed services as well as the ranks of industrial workers during the war, contributing to the war effort in important ways. But wherever they went, they faced racist policies, segregation, harassment, poor pay, and the worst jobs. Although wartime offered some improvement for impoverished blacks, the system of segregation prevented them from reaping the same benefits as

their white counterparts. The reality of wartime left many blacks feeling bitter. "No one does anything—you never get anything—out of the goodness of people's hearts," said one black woman who had worked in a wartime munitions factory.

African Americans learned that they would have to fight for their own rights. As early as 1940, at a civil rights convention in Chicago, a black woman delegate suggested, "We ought to throw fifty thousand Negroes around the White House, bring them from all over the country, in jalopies, in trains and any way they can get there . . . until we get some action from the White House." She was calling for integration of the defense industries, where blacks were segregated into the worst jobs with the lowest pay. The very threat of such a demonstration proved to be effective: President Roosevelt issued Executive Order 8802, which outlawed discriminatory hiring

Scalers work on the S.S. George Washington Carver at the Kaiser Shipyards in Richmond, California. Black women, though highly skilled, were often assigned to the dirtiest industrial tasks.

practices by defense contractors and established the Committee on Fair Employment Practices.

More than half a million African Americans migrated out of the rural South during the war to work in defense industries. But racial tensions worsened as competition for jobs and housing between blacks and whites exploded in urban riots in New York City, Detroit, and other cities. Even in the armed services, where black men served just as willingly and courageously as white men, blacks were subjected to verbal and physical attacks by their white counterparts. Nevertheless, the armed forces, like the war industries, provided steady income throughout the war.

Women were among the thousands of African Americans who migrated to northern cities during the war to work in industry. Lillian Hatcher was one of the first black women to be hired above the service level in the Detroit auto industry, and her new job in the factory paid her twice what she was earning previously as a cafeteria worker. She later recalled,

> I was working not for patriotic reasons, I was working for the money. The 97 cents an hour was the greatest salary that I had earned. Going up to $1.16 an hour—that was going to be my top rate. And I really needed that money, because my son was wearing out corduroy pants, two and three pair a month, gym shoes and all the other things my daughters too had to have, you know, clothing and shoes and all that stuff. And our house rent was the whole price of $32.50 a month and we had to save for that, in order to pay $32.50 and keep the light and gas.

African Americans had to fight for the jobs they wanted. Poet Maya Angelou became the first black streetcar conductor in San Francisco during the war, but not without a struggle. She made herself a promise that "made my veins stand out, and my mouth tighten into a prune: I WOULD HAVE THE JOB. I WOULD BE A CONDUCTORETTE AND SLING A FULL MONEY CHANGER FROM MY BELT. I WOULD." And she did.

Many were not as fortunate as Angelou to get the job of their choice. Black women in wartime industries were given the most dangerous jobs in the factories. In airplane assembly plants, black women worked in the "dope rooms" filled with poisonous fumes of glue, while white women were in the well-ventilated sewing rooms. In every industry, the lowest paying, most difficult, most dangerous,

hottest, and most uncomfortable jobs went to black women—and they often worked the night shifts. Sarah Killingsworth, an African-American woman working in a Los Angeles defense plant, came from Tennessee where she made $2.50 a week. In her new job, she earned $40 a week, even though she had the most menial of jobs: tending the ladies' rest room during the night shift. But she did not find the work itself oppressive. Rather, she saw it as a way to help other women workers.

"I would give them a No-Doz so they could stay awake all night," Killingsworth recalled. "This was the graveyard shift. Some of 'em had been out drinkin', and we would let them take a nap for about fifteen minutes. We would watch out for them, so their supervisor wouldn't miss 'em. We put the sign out: Closed. We'd wake 'em up, and sometimes they'd give us tips. They would give me fifty cents for a tablet or a cup of coffee, so they could stay awake. Especially on weekends." Overall, she believed the war benefited black people. "They didn't mix the white and black in the war. But now it gives you a kind of independence because they felt that we gone off and

Black women staff a civil defense message center in Washington, D.C., dispatching first aid and other emergency services workers throughout the city.

Black dance clubs and other cultural activities sprang up in the cities where African Americans clustered to take jobs in wartime industry.

fought, we should be equal. Everything started openin' up for us. We got a chance to go places we had never been able to go before."

New opportunities emerged for African-American women not only in the factories, but in the growing black communities as well. In Richmond, California, for example, black migration contributed to the transformation of a small town into a bustling metropolis. Before the war, there were only 270 blacks in Richmond. But when the city became a war production center, African Americans from the South came there to work in the shipyards. By 1943 the black population had increased by 5,000 percent. Slightly more than half of the southern black migrants to Richmond during the war were women.

The presence of blacks was apparent not only in the factories, but in the social and cultural life of the city, most notably in the blues clubs that began to proliferate. Many of these clubs were owned and operated by African-American women who had migrated to Richmond from Arkansas. One such female entrepreneur was Margaret Starks, manager of Tappers Inn, the most popular club in North Richmond. Starks also served as a talent booking agent for a number of local clubs and published the city's first black newspaper on the premises of the Tappers Inn.

Margaret Starks's business acumen fed into her political activities, and she served as the secretary of the Richmond branch of the NAACP during the war years. Along with the newspaper, she also located the NAACP offices in a room at Tappers. "Everybody would know where to find me if they needed any [business] done," she said, explaining the various activities she ran out of the inn. Women like Margaret Starks, and the blues club scene they helped to create, provided an arena where African-American people exerted some power over their lives and developed community institutions. In spite of the city's official discrimination and segregation policies, within the African-American community blacks could organize politically and form networks for their own social and economic needs.

Like African Americans and Native Americans, Mexicans and Mexican Americans had long been isolated from mainstream American society and segregated into menial jobs. Mexican women in the Southwest were overwhelmingly segregated in garment and food-processing firms. During World War II, however, women took advantage of the wartime demand for their labor to advance their interests. The activism of women working at the California Sanitary Canning Company provides one dramatic example. Energetic labor organizers like Luisa Moreno and Dorothy Ray Healy built a powerful union of women workers who were able to achieve a wage increase and recognition of their union. Family and community networks helped support and strengthen the union. Although their union could not be sustained after the war in the face of mounting opposition by anti-Communist crusaders, the successes of this union during the war demonstrate how much control these women were able to achieve over their work lives.

Seventy-five percent of all workers in the California canneries were women. Because women formed the majority, their segregation from male employees allowed women to work in the plants in an atmosphere of little interference from men. In other industries

In 1943, Luisa Moreno (far left) served on the union committee that negotiated with the California Sanitary Canning Company for better wages and working conditions for Mexicana workers.

where men were in the majority, however, the segregation of women was a disadvantage. Automobile manufacturing, for example, remained male dominated. Before the war, women accounted for only 10 percent of all auto workers, where they were concentrated in a relatively small number of jobs. After an initial shutdown, the industry retooled for war production. When the plant doors reopened in 1942, male workers were in short supply and women were hired in unprecedented numbers. By the end of 1943, a fourth of the industry's workers were female.

Throughout the war, although the boundaries continued to shift as new definitions of "women's work" were required, the automobile industry maintained women in certain jobs and men in others. Despite the dramatic upswing in women's participation in the work force, unions had not developed strategies that included a place for women's concerns in their negotiations with the companies, nor had a strong feminist movement come together to assert women's needs, such as child care and equal access to good jobs. As a result, gender division of labor survived the war.

In spite of women's dramatic contributions to the war effort, they were not able to achieve equal pay or working conditions. Their unequal treatment led to a campaign for equal rights. The Republicans in 1940 and the Democrats in 1944 supported the Equal Rights

Amendment (ERA), but the two major union federations, the American Federation of Labor (AFL) and the Congress of Industrial Organizations (CIO), opposed it. Even Frances Perkins, secretary of labor, and Eleanor Roosevelt, first lady—two activists on behalf of women's rights—refused to support the legislation because they feared that women workers would lose legal protections against long hours and health hazards. In 1945, Congress considered a bill that would have required equal pay for women. But even with a fair amount of bipartisan support, and some union backing, that measure failed. When the ERA finally reached the Senate in 1946, it received less than the two-thirds majority necessary to pass, although a majority of senators voted for it.

Frances Perkins was the first woman cabinet member, serving as Franklin Roosevelt's secretary of labor from 1933 to 1945. She advocated equal wages for women and men and urged industries to keep doors open to women workers after the war.

All of these measures met defeat in large part because women's war work was expected to end. The War Manpower Commission assumed that "the separation of women from industry should flow in an orderly plan." Frederick Crawford, head of the National Association of Manufacturers, found a point of agreement with his usual adversaries, the union leaders, when he said, "From a humanitarian point of view, too many women should not stay in the labor force. The home is the basic American institution." Many women rejected this notion. As one argued, "War jobs have uncovered unsuspected abilities in American women. Why lose all these abilities because of a belief that 'a woman's place is in the home'? For some it is, for others not." But her words would be drowned in a sea of voices calling upon women to prepare to assume their places in the kitchens and bedrooms of returning servicemen.

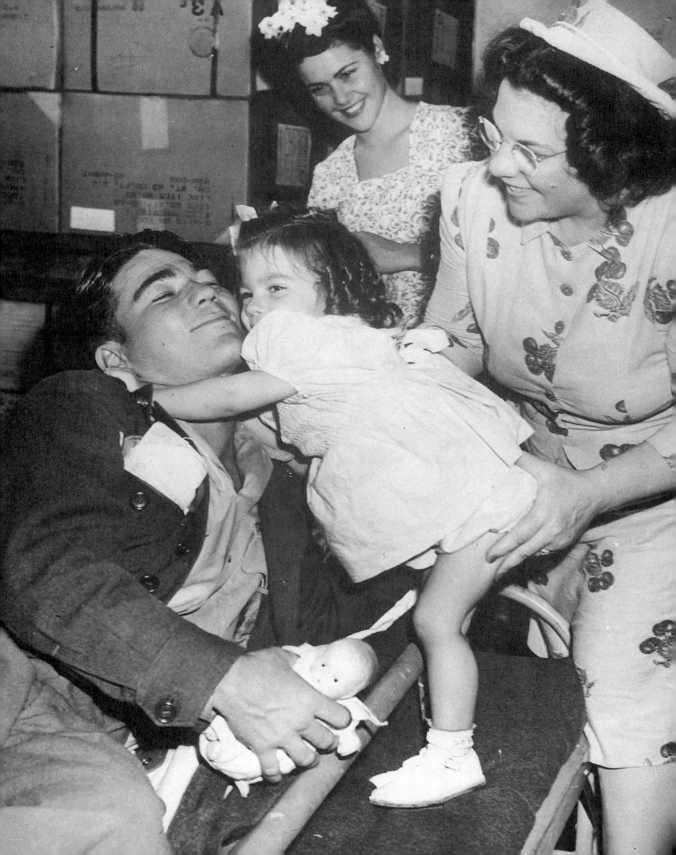

CHAPTER 3

WINDING DOWN: SIGNS POINT TO HOME

During the war, as women streamed into the paid labor force, some observers feared that women might not be willing to settle down into family life once the emergency ended. Perhaps these anxieties emerged because the war years brought a noticeable number of women into occupations previously reserved for men. In addition, the war removed men from the home front, demonstrating that women could manage quite well without them. Single women now became targets of campaigns that would continue after the war, urging women back into their domestic roles.

Single women also caused alarm because of their perceived or potential sexual activity. A typical wartime pamphlet warned, "The war in general has given women new status, new recognition. . . . Women are 'coming into their own' in this war. . . . Yet it is essential that women avoid arrogance and retain their femininity in the face of their own new status. . . . In her new independence she must not lose her humanness as a woman. She may be the woman of the moment, but she must watch her moments."

This theme echoed throughout the war. One college textbook for family life courses, *Marriage and the Family* (1940), explained why women had to watch their moments so carefully:

Homecoming 1945: Three joyous women greet the man of the family, who was wounded in the invasion of Normandy.

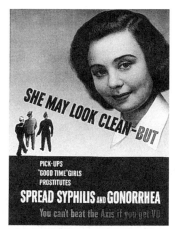

Government posters warned veterans of the dangers of venereal diseases: The one at top suggests a careful choice of female companions. In the bottom poster, VD (shown as a woman) was compared to the archenemies of America, the fascist dictators Hitler and Tojo.

[T]he greater social freedom of women has more or less inevitably led to a greater degree of sexual laxity, a freedom which strikes at the heart of family stability.... When women work, earn, and spend as much as men do, they are going to ask for equal rights with men. But the right to behave like a man meant [sic] also the right to misbehave as he does. The decay of established moralities came about as a by-product.

In this remarkable passage, the authors of the textbook state as if it were a scientific formula their opinion that social freedom and employment for women would cause "sexual laxity," moral decay, and the destruction of the family.

Writers like these urged women to stay "pure" for the soon-to-be-returning veterans. At the same time, they warned soldiers to avoid sexual contact with women who hung around army bases to prevent catching venereal diseases from them. Wartime purity crusades marked a revision of the germ theory: germs were not responsible for spreading disease; "promiscuous" women were. Widely distributed posters warned that even the angelic "girl next door" might carry disease. "She may look clean, but ...," read one caption next to a picture of everybody's sweetheart. Wartime ushered in an anxious preoccupation with all forms of nonmarital sexuality. It ranged from concern about prostitution to fierce campaigns against homosexuals and other so-called "deviants" in military as well as civilian life.

Although the alarmists' fears were exaggerated, it was true that wartime opened up new possibilities for sexual experimentation. More young people moved into cities and away from neighborhood and parental supervision. Many now earned their own money and took charge of their own leisure time and behavior. For many young women experiencing this new independence, men in uniform held special appeal. "When I was sixteen," recalled a college student a few years later, "I let a sailor pick me up and go all the way with me. I had intercourse with him partly because he had a strong personal appeal for me, but mainly because I had a feeling of high adventure and because I wanted to please a member of the armed forces." With so many girls in this adventurous spirit, one teenage boy described wartime as "a real sex paradise. The plant and the town were just full of working girls who were on the make. Where I was, a male war worker became the center of loose morality."

New recruits to the WAVES, the women's branch of the navy, arrive for basic training at Great Lakes, Illinois. Women proudly served in the navy during World War II, performing intelligence, administrative, and other crucial functions.

While women were encouraged to enter the paid labor force, wartime changes in women's behavior aroused concern. Nowhere was this ambivalence more obvious than in the military itself. In a major change from the past, women entered every part of military service except combat. One thousand civilian female pilots joined the Women's Airforce Service Pilots (WASP), 140,000 women joined the Women's Army Corps (WAC), 100,000 entered the navy as WAVES (Women Accepted for Voluntary Emergency Service), and others enlisted with the marines and coast guard. A few were physicians, and many were nurses. Although a small number of women held dramatic and highly publicized positions in formerly all-male areas such as aviation, most served in administrative, clerical, and communications jobs. Occupations in the military reflected the gender-based divisions in the civilian labor force.

Nevertheless, the military made great efforts to recruit women during the war. Oveta Culp Hobby, director of the Women's Army Corps, proclaimed women "are carrying on the glorious tradition of American womanhood. They are making history! . . . This is a war which recognizes no distinctions between men and women." To the female Americans she hoped to recruit, she said, "This is

Oveta Culp Hobby was director of the Women's Army Corps (WACs) during World War II. Thousands of young women heeded her call to join the military.

YOUR war." Women of "excellent character" who could pass an intelligence test could join the WACs, provided they had no children under the age of 14. Healthy, unmarried women with no dependents under the age of 18 could enlist in the WAVES. A WAVE who married might remain in the service, if she had finished basic training and as long as her husband was not in the service. The birth of a child brought an "honorable discharge."

Although the armed forces offered women alternatives to full-time homemaking, it was virtually impossible to combine a job in the military with family life. Nevertheless, the armed services presented the image of the female recruit as very "feminine" and domestically inclined. Every effort was made to dispel prevailing notions that military work would make women "masculine" or ruin their moral character. A guidebook for women in the armed services

and war industries, for example, included a photograph of a young WAVE with a caption that described her as "pretty as her picture . . . in the trim uniform that enlisted U.S. Navy Waves will wear in winter . . . smartly-styled, comfortable uniforms . . . with a soft rolled-brim hat." Women in the military were needed for their "delicate hands" and "precision work at which women are so adept," and in hospitals where "there is a need in a man for comfort and attention that only a woman can fill." Women's corps leaders did little to challenge these images; they assured the public that after the war enlisted women would be "as likely as other women to make marriage their profession."

These publicity measures met with only partial success amid public sentiment suspicious of women in nontraditional roles. In fact, rumors about the supposedly promiscuous sexual behavior and scandalous drunkenness of female recruits were so widespread that the armed forces had to refute the charges publicly. One result was to make into policy the sexual double standard in the military: men were routinely supplied with contraceptives (mainly to prevent the spread of venereal disease), but women were denied access to birth control devices. In the rare cases in which sexual transgressions were discovered, women were punished more severely than men.

Lesbianism was another reality of wartime that the military took pains to suppress. But the military was an ideal place for lesbian relationships to flourish. Phillis Abry quit her job as a lab technician to join the WACs because she "wanted to be with all those women." Homosexuality was not allowed in the military, of course, but lesbians were not easily identified. "I remember being very nervous about them asking me if I had any homosexual feelings or attitudes," she recalled. "I just smiled and was sweet and feminine."

At the same time that women's war work was given a domestic aura, domestic tasks gained new patriotic purpose. Millions of women were involved in volunteer work during the war, and much of it involved traditional skills such as canning, saving cooking fats, and making household goods last longer. Much as homemakers in the depression recognized the importance of their domestic skills for the survival of their families during the economic emergency, so the homemakers of the war years saw their work as contributing to the success of the war emergency.

Women contributed to the war effort, but not at the expense of their domestic duties. Traditional marriage was still expected for women. It was, in fact, one of the primary reasons given for fighting

Women on the home front served their country with domestic skills: packing cookies for shipment to servicemen overseas and canning food for use at home.

the war. The walls of barracks were decorated with "pinups," photographs of women in alluring poses reminding the men why they were fighting. Movie star Betty Grable was the most popular pinup, not because she was the most sexy and glamorous, but because she had a rather wholesome look. Grable came to represent the girl back home and the "American Way of Life" that inspired the men to fight. As one soldier wrote in a letter to Grable, "There we were out in those damn dirty trenches. Machine guns firing. Bombs dropping all around us. We would be exhausted, frightened, confused, and sometimes hopeless about our situation. When suddenly someone would pull your picture out of his wallet. Or we'd see a decal of you on a plane and then we'd know what we were fighting for."

Grable became even more popular when she married band leader Harry James in 1943 and had a child later that year. It reinforced her image as everyone's sweetheart, future wife, and mother. In order to be worthy of similar adoration, women sent their husbands and sweethearts photos of themselves in "pinup" poses. Betty Grable herself encouraged women to send their men photos of themselves in swimsuits, to inspire them to fight on and come home to an erotically charged marriage. Men at war were encouraged to fantasize about sex that awaited them when they returned—not with the "victory girls" who hung around bases, but with their wives. In the words of one soldier, "We are not only fighting for the Four Freedoms, we are fighting also for the priceless privilege of making love to American women."

The popular culture was filled with many such messages. One example, produced under government sponsorship, was a series of programs aired on all major radio networks in 1942 in an effort to mobilize support for the war. One highly acclaimed segment, "To The Young," included this exhortation:

Young Male Voice: "That's one of the things this war's about."

Young Female Voice: "About us?"

Young Male Voice: "About *all* young people like us. About love and gettin' hitched, and havin' a home and some kids, and breathin' fresh air out in the suburbs . . . about livin' an' workin' *decent*, like free people."

The sleeping quarters for sailors at Guadalcanal demonstrate the art of the pinup: the walls are covered with photos of alluring women.

*This mother of twins demon-
strates the ideal of domestic
bliss in the war years.*

Americans conformed to this expectation. Women entered war production, but they did not give up on reproduction. The war brought a dramatic reversal in patterns of family formation of the 1930s. The depression was marked by delayed marriages and declining marriage and birthrates, yet more than 1 million more families formed between 1940 and 1943 than would have been expected during normal times. The marriage rate was spurred by the draft deferment for married men in the early war years, and also by the imminence of departure for foreign shores. During the war the birthrate also jumped, from 19.4 to 24.5 births per 1,000 population.

In the popular culture, we find these same patterns. The most popular motion picture of the 1930s was *Gone with the Wind,* a story of the survival during hard times of a shrewd and tough woman whose domestic life ends up in shambles, but the top box office hit of wartime was quite different. The 1944 government-sponsored war propaganda film *This Is the Army,* starring Ronald Reagan, was the most successful film of the war years. In this film, the men are center stage as they finish the job their fathers began in World War I. The plot revolves around the efforts of the central character's sweetheart to persuade her reluctant soldier to marry her. Finally she succeeds, and the duo wed just before the hero leaves to fight overseas.

Along with the wifely focus of the 1940s came a move away

from the flamboyant sexuality that characterized major stars of the 1920s and '30s. Bette Davis, noted for her strong-minded independence in the '30s, proclaimed in 1941 that it was still "a man's world in spite of the fact that girls have pretty much invaded it." Therefore, women must protect the most precious thing they have: their reputations. For modern women still want what grandma wanted: "a great love, a happy home, a peaceful old age." Do not be afraid to be termed a "prude," said Davis. "Good sports are dated every night of the week—prudes are saved for special dates. Good sports get plenty of rings on the telephone, but prudes get them on the finger. Men take good sports *out*—they take prudes home—yes, right home to Mother and Dad and all the neighbors." These, then, were the mixed messages of wartime. Women should shoulder their share of the war effort, but keep their goals focused on the home.

In spite of all the limitations, women took advantage of every new opportunity available to them. Perhaps the most dramatic example of this resourcefulness can be seen in the experiences of Japanese-American women during World War II. More than any other

The crucial wedding scene in the popular 1940 feature This Is the Army, *starring Ronald Reagan. The movie's theme reinforced the ideal of home and family during wartime.*

group of American citizens, Japanese Americans suffered during the war. Following the bombing of Pearl Harbor on December 7, 1941, the United States and Japan were at war. Immediately, a wave of suspicion and hostility toward Japanese and Japanese-Americans surfaced, especially on the West Coast, where their presence was considered a threat to national security. On February 19, 1942, President Franklin Roosevelt signed Executive Order 9066, which suspended the civil rights of American citizens of Japanese descent by authorizing the removal of 110,000 Japanese and their American-born children from western states.

Families were given one week's notice to evacuate their homes and move to assembly centers, 14 hastily-constructed, prisonlike compounds in California, Oregon, and Washington. Many citizens lived in these camps for the duration of the war. Some left in order to serve in the armed forces, attend college, work nearby, or relocate to the East. But all were profoundly affected by the disruptions in their lives and the hardships they faced in the camps. As one woman wrote from a camp in 1942, "The life here cannot be expressed. Sometimes, we are resigned to it, but when we see the barbed wire fences and the sentry tower with floodlights, it gives us a feeling of being prisoners in a 'concentration camp.' We try to be happy and yet oftentimes a gloominess does creep in. . . . I just wonder if all the sacrifices and hard labor on [the] part of our parents has gone up to leave nothing to show for it?"

In spite of the extreme hardships and humiliations of internment, the loss of liberty, privacy, and comforts, Japanese-American women made the best of the situation, and even managed to gain some benefits from it. The intimacy of the camps posed a challenge to formal patterns of arranged marriage, and young women asserted more freedom of choice to date and marry whomever they wished. Because most people had access to a wide range of jobs in the camps, young women were able to experiment with a variety of occupations, ranging from mess-hall work to accounting to optometry. Many took advantage of opportunities to go to college.

World War II opened up new opportunities for women, but it also imposed many constraints. The war extended the state of crisis that characterized the depression, and disrupted expected activities for women and men. Yet many women liked the new freedom they

A Japanese-American family prepares for relocation to a detention center in May 1942. This sorrowful image was captured in Turlock, California, by the noted documentary photographer Dorothea Lange, who was then working for the government.

gained during the war, the challenging, well-paying jobs, and the chance to demonstrate their abilities. As the *New York Times Magazine* noted near the end of the war:

> Alma goes to work because she wants to go to work. She wants to go now and she wants to keep going when the war is over. Alma's had a taste of LIFE. She's poked her head out into the one-man's world. . . . Of course, all the Alma's haven't thought through why they want to work after the war or how it's going to be possible. But they have gone far enough to know that they can do whatever is required in a machine shop. They've had the pleasure of feeling money in their pockets—money they've earned themselves.

But Alma was in for a rude awakening after the war. She was unlikely to be able to keep that well-paying job in the machine shop she so enjoyed. Although the vast majority of women who worked for wages during the war wanted to keep their jobs, many lost their wartime positions to the returning veterans. Men and women alike were expected to relinquish their emergency roles and settle into domestic life—men as breadwinners, women as homemakers. In this vision, there was no room for the independent single woman, nor the married career woman. After the war, all the major institutions in which Americans lived and worked came to foster the vision of a nation finding its ultimate security in the traditional American home.

A young mother wheels her baby along a makeshift sidewalk in a veterans' trailer park in Charlottesville, Virginia.

Many returning soldiers and their wives began their postwar lives in veterans' housing assembled from surplus Quonset huts reminiscent of their service barracks.

CHAPTER 4

DOMESTICITY:
THE NUCLEAR FAMILY
IN THE NUCLEAR AGE

I n the summer of 1959, a young couple married and spent their honeymoon in a bomb shelter. *Life* magazine featured the peculiar adventure and quipped that "fallout can be fun." Although the "sheltered honeymoon" was little more than a publicity stunt, it serves as an eerie symbol of the nuclear family in the nuclear age. The young couple, surrounded by consumer goods, spent two weeks in total isolation, protected from the world by the thick concrete walls of a 22-ton steel and concrete box, 12 feet underground. In many ways, the shelter represents the family itself: sealed off from the dangers of the world.

As soon as World War II ended in 1945, the Cold War began. The United States had dropped two nuclear bombs on Japanese cities, ushering in the Atomic Age. The cloud created by those massive explosions lingered in the world's consciousness for decades. Within a few years, the Soviet Union exploded its first atomic bomb, and the arms race between the two superpowers began in earnest. Elsewhere in the world the Chinese revolution overturned a government friendly to the United States and replaced it with a Communist regime. This was quickly followed by Communist North Korea's invasion of South Korea. At home, a fierce crusade against communism led to mass hysteria in which almost anyone who dared to criticize the U.S. government might be labeled a subversive. The peace

Mother knits as Father reads "Cinderella" to their daughters (and a squirming dog). This photo was used in a life insurance public relations campaign to promote the ideal of the nuclear family.

During the Cold War of the 1950s and early 1960s, Americans built fallout shelters outfitted with bedding and canned food for the entire family.

Americans welcomed after 1945 was a fragile one at best.

The woman in the "sheltered honeymoon" was a far cry from "Rosie the Riveter." Gone was the popular wartime icon in her goggles and overalls using heavy equipment to put together a battleship. For American women, the end of the war brought nearly as many changes as wartime itself. Many had to leave their well-paying wartime jobs to make room for the returning veterans. Nearly all the "Rosies" who had riveted had to find something else to do. Many continued to work in the postwar years, often in occupations that did not pay as well. But whether employed or not, nearly all women, and nearly all men, caught the family fever.

During the years after World War II, Americans were more eager than ever to establish families. The family became the ultimate symbol of security for Americans tired of depression and war. As world tensions loomed while the United States and the Soviet Union viewed each other with suspicion and hostility, families could feel safe inside the walls of their houses. They could also feel economically secure with the stable salaries male breadwinners were able to earn in the booming postwar economy. The bomb-shelter honeymooners were part of a generation who lowered the age at marriage for both men and women, and quickly brought the birthrate to a

20th-century high after more than a hundred years of steady decline. This produced the famous "Baby Boom" that lasted for two decades.

The divorce rate also declined, after a postwar peak in 1946 (caused, no doubt, by the dissolution of hasty wartime marriages). This peculiar pattern of young marriage, high birthrate, and low divorce was one of the most striking features of the postwar years, and it ended as abruptly as it began. It lasted only until the Baby Boom children came of age. By the late 1960s, the nation had returned to long-term trends: lower birthrates and higher divorce rates. The 1940s and 1950s stand out as unique: a 20-year era of domesticity.

The rush into family life was accompanied by a powerful belief in the idea of "togetherness." *McCall's* magazine celebrated this family ethic in 1954 when it proclaimed to its white middle-class readers that women were marrying younger, raising larger families, and living in affluent homes. "But the most impressive and the most heartening feature of this change is that men, women, and children are achieving it together. They are creating this new and warmer way of life not as women alone or men alone, isolated from one another, but as a family sharing a common experience."

The Baby Boom affected nearly everyone. The postwar era appeared on the surface to be a time of mass conformity, when most

This Georgia farmer credited his prosperity, and his ability to raise a large family, to his training in Future Farmers of America.

people seemed to dress alike, behave alike, vote alike, and share common values. But there were deep divisions in society, particularly along racial lines. Yet when it came to having babies, everyone was doing it. If we divide the population according to economic class, religion, racial identification, or any other category, we find that among all groups the birthrate rose in the 1940s and '50s and then declined in the 1960s. The Baby Boom was a statistical indicator of the intense focus on family life that permeated the nation in the years after World War II.

This powerful commitment to family was accompanied by a widely held belief that men should be the wage earners for their families, and women should tend to the home and children. Women of all racial, ethnic, and class backgrounds faced intense pressure to become wives and mothers after the war, and to make homemaking their primary career. Agnes Meyer expressed these sentiments in 1950 when she wrote in the *Atlantic Monthly*, "What modern woman has to recapture is the wisdom that just being a woman is her central task and greatest honor. . . . Women must boldly announce that no job is more exacting, more necessary, or more rewarding than that of housewife and mother." But working women were not eager to leave the labor force. Four out of five women who worked during the war hoped to keep working after the war, including 69 percent of working wives.

Although more than 3 million women left their wartime jobs, most were rehired into other occupations. By 1947, there were more

This image epitomizes the 1950s ideal of the nuclear family: white-collar father supporting a wife absorbed in her child and domestic activities.

women in the paid labor force than there had been during the war, and more working wives than ever before. Somehow, home life would have to respond to the increasing number of employed married women. But the policies of the government, private sector employers, and even labor unions made it difficult for women to avoid economic dependence on their husbands or their fathers even if they continued to hold jobs. Although it was still possible for most women who wanted a job to find one, these jobs rarely paid well. Women's average weekly pay declined from $50 to $37, a drop of 26 percent, more than five times the postwar decrease for men. Three quarters of the women who had jobs in war industries were still employed after the war, but 90 percent of them were earning less than they had during the war.

Women also left the military. Public opinion was no longer so willing to tolerate "unfeminine" military occupations for women now that the war was over. But female veterans faced particular

Typists transcribe dictation in a government office staffed entirely by women. Most working women during the war and in the following decade held clerical and other nonprofessional jobs.

hardships. Fewer than half were able to find jobs that made use of the skills they learned during the war. To make matters worse, they were not eligible for many of the important veterans' benefits available to their male counterparts, such as homeowner's loans.

In spite of the huge numbers of women in the paid labor force, female employees found it difficult to combine the responsibilities of a family with a job outside the home. The few child care facilities that had been established by the federal government during the war closed, and mothers of small children faced even more intense pressures to stay home. As younger women left the paid labor force in order to have babies, they made room for older women whose children were in school.

It was not unusual for women to take jobs after their children were grown. Since most women married young and had their children during their early 20s, they were in their mid-30s when their youngest child entered school. With the life span increasing, many women could look forward to decades of active life when their primary childrearing duties were over. Since very few highly skilled, well-paying, or professional positions were available, most of these

Many women worked in so-called pink-collar jobs, such as food service. These efficient women operated rolling food carts that enabled a New Jersey factory to feed its workers lunch in a mere 20 minutes.

women took jobs as secretaries, clerks, saleswomen, and waitresses in the "pink-collar ghetto," poorly paying service jobs held almost exclusively by women. As a result of these expanding job opportunities, the number of employed women continued to rise after the war, even though the range of employment available to them narrowed.

Black women were hit especially hard by the changes in the female labor force. Although they experienced a slight overall gain, their income was still less than half that of white women at the end of the 1940s. The gains of wartime largely vanished for African Americans, and the racism they faced felt especially bitter after all they had sacrificed for the country. In 1945, Maya Angelou noted with sadness that former black war heroes were now "hanging on the ghetto corners like forgotten laundry left on a back yard fence. . . . Thus we lived through a major war. The question in the ghettos was, Can we make it through a minor peace?"

Ruth Shays was a domestic servant who noted cynically that the slight respect she was accorded by her white employer during wartime vanished after the war. "You see, these Japanese and Germans was threatening to cut their toenails too short to walk, so she called herself being friendly by not using that word 'nigger' because she knows I hate and despise it. . . . Whenever they get a little scared they try to act like they might be decent, but when that war was over you didn't hear much about freedom and the equal rights, and what you heard didn't have much to do with what was going on."

Although wartime brought both black and white women into the paid labor force in record numbers, jobs remained divided according to race. By 1950, although the numbers of black women employed as domestic servants had declined, 60 percent of all employed black women still worked as maids in private homes or as service workers in institutions, compared to only 16 percent of white working women. In contrast, 40 percent of employed white women held clerical jobs as secretaries, clerks, and saleswomen, compared to only 5 percent of black women.

As a result of these differences, black women and white women faced very different choices after the war. White women might decide to forgo paid employment and marry a man with a well-paying job, taking on the role of full-time homemaker and mother in a com-

Many black women in both the North and South found work as domestic servants in the homes of wealthy whites.

fortable suburban home. Black women did not have that choice. Excluded from the suburbs, married to men who faced poorly paid jobs and few chances for advancement, they had to develop different strategies. As one black woman explained, after the war their families were "crammed on top of each other—jammed and packed and forced into the smallest possible space." As they had before as well as during the war, black women continued to seek whatever employment they could get.

For many white women, the need for extra household income made it acceptable to take jobs they enjoyed and gain a respite from household tasks. Married women's wages helped purchase the appliances, automobiles, and other consumer goods that became available in the expanding postwar economy. By 1960, 10 million wives were employed—triple the number in 1940—but fewer than half of them worked full time. Most of these positions were jobs, not careers. In spite of the return to prosperity, there were proportionately fewer women in professions than there had been in 1930.

According to polls taken at the time, half of employed women claimed to be working "to buy something," and only one fifth admitted to "a need for accomplishment." These women were supposed to be working to benefit their families, not themselves. If they said they enjoyed their jobs, they might have appeared selfish. At the same time, many women faced the stress of "double duty," coming home from work to face household responsibilities. Nevertheless, 60 percent said that they found self-esteem in their jobs. For young married women with children at home, the strain of holding a job may not have been worth the meager rewards. But for older married women, a job was an acceptable alternative to the full-time homemaker role, and contributed to the family income as well.

The shrinking job opportunities for women after the war reflected more than efforts to keep women "in their place," at home. Just as important was the need to preserve a place for men. The economic depression of the 1930s had barely lifted before men who were in the prime of their working lives were again wrenched from their jobs. Many of the more than 16 million men who served in the armed forces during the war wondered if they would be unemployed when they returned. Wartime surveys revealed deep fears about postwar life: 7 out of 10 Americans expected to be worse off after the war, 6 out of 10 anticipated lower wages, and three fourths believed there would be fewer jobs. Many business leaders expected a major depression with high unemployment within a decade. *Fortune* maga-

A New York taxi driver signs up for the International Brotherhood of Teamsters in 1955. At that time there were only 55 women cab drivers in New York City.

Veterans in Trenton, New Jersey, attend a special class in English literature. The government also provided training in construction and other vocational skills.

zine summed it up: "The American soldier is depression conscious … worried sick about post-war joblessness."

Although the economy turned out to be much healthier than these pessimistic wartime predictions, returning veterans nevertheless faced many difficulties. Thousands of men were unemployed in the immediate postwar years, costing the government $2.5 billion in unemployment benefits. There was also a severe housing shortage, forcing many families to double up in cramped quarters. Along with these difficulties were the physical and psychic scars of war. More than half of the veterans who saw social workers for counseling were treated for psychological distress caused by their combat experiences.

Under the circumstances, few begrudged the advantages given to former servicemen, who were considered to be the nation's heroes. They received housing loans, educational benefits, and medical care. Most of the veterans' benefits were geared toward men, not to women who had served in the armed services. Female veterans, like their civilian sisters, were expected to become wives and mothers after the war. It was widely believed that they would best serve the needs of the returning soldiers by becoming their wives and the mothers of their children, rather than by competing with them for jobs and training programs. As one marriage counselor put it in a statement addressed to wives and future brides of returning servicemen: "Let him know you now want him to take charge."

The generous benefits available to returning veterans became known as the GI Bill of Rights, or simply the GI Bill. (GI was an abbreviation for "government issue," and was often used to refer to soldiers.) Among the most noteworthy features of the GI Bill were educational benefits. Nearly half of all veterans, more than 6 million men, flooded into colleges, universities, and other training programs. By 1947, nearly half of all college students were veterans. College enrollments also increased for women during the postwar years, but not at the same rate as for men.

Although more women were enrolled than before, they represented a smaller percentage of the student population. Women had made up 47 percent of college students in 1920; by 1958 they were only 35 percent of the total, and they earned fewer degrees. During the war years, some barriers to women were removed. Harvard Medical

In the 1950s, veterans filled colleges and universities across the country. Their education was paid for by the GI Bill.

School, for example, finally admitted women for the first time in 1945. But as professional opportunities for women shrank, so did the number of advanced degrees they earned. College and professional degrees did not guarantee the same entry into well-paying jobs and careers for women as they did for men. As a result, more than half of all women college students dropped out in order to marry and become housewives, or to support husbands through school.

In 1945, these 12 graduates of prestigious colleges became the first women to be admitted to Harvard Medical School.

Jokes at the time reflected this trend: women were often said to be pursuing an "MRS. degree," since so many met their future husbands in college and then dropped out to marry and have children. Another term reflected a different pattern: women earning their "Ph.T.," or Putting Hubby Through, were holding jobs while their husbands completed college. It was expected that a college-educated man could get a better job than a college-educated woman, and would be able to support his family after graduation.

In terms of education, as in many other areas of life, there were striking differences in opportunities and experiences according to one's race. Educational differences between black women and white

Women attend a lecture at Vassar College. Many teachers at all-women's colleges believed that their students' main goals should be marriage and motherhood.

women were particularly striking. One study showed that young women in an all-white sample were twice as likely to enter college as their mothers had been, but were much less likely to complete their degrees. Instead, they were much more likely to marry highly educated men. Only 37 percent of women college students completed their degrees. It is not likely that the women who dropped out of school did so because they were unable to handle the rigors of academic life. Nor did they simply give up. Rather, they were following the advice of many of their teachers, and considering their opportunities for the future.

In 1949, the noted sociologist Talcott Parsons told his students at Radcliffe College that "the woman's fundamental status is that of her husband's wife, the mother of his children." Many undoubtedly took such advice to heart. According to one white woman who graduated from Radcliffe in 1951 and went on to become the wife of a college dean, "We married what we wanted to *be*. If we wanted to be a lawyer or a doctor we married one." In other words, college enabled these white women to find and marry men who had good occupational prospects.

In 1956, presidential candidate Adlai Stevenson spoke to Smith College graduates at their commencement ceremonies, urging them to take up the banner of domesticity with pride: "Once they wrote poetry. Now it's the laundry list. Once they discussed art and philosophy until late in the night. Now they are so tired they fall asleep as soon as the dishes are finished." But "women in the home [can] have an important political influence on man and boy.... I think there is much you can do about our crisis in the humble role of housewife. I could wish you no better vocation than that." For many white college-educated women, that indeed would be their fate.

For black women, the pattern was very different. Since most black women expected to be employed, like their mothers and grandmothers before them, college degrees would greatly improve their occupational prospects. Although there were far fewer black women than white women in college, more than 90 percent of black women who entered college completed their degrees.

Pauli Murray, born into an African-American family in the South, struggled against the double burdens of race and sex. Coming from a long line of activists, she was determined to devote her life to the plight of the sharecroppers of her home region and other disadvantaged blacks. In 1941 she entered Howard Law School, the elite school for African Americans at the time. Although she was spared racism at the historically black institution, she ran into her first brush with sexism there. "Ironically," she later wrote, "if Howard Law School equipped me for effective struggle against Jim Crow [the system of racial segregation], it was also the place where I first became conscious of the twin evil of discriminatory sex bias, which I quickly labeled Jane Crow."

Although the men were friendly, sexism took an insidious form. "I soon learned that women were often the objects of ridicule disguised as a joke. I was shocked on the first day of class when one of our professors said in his opening remarks that he really didn't know why women came to law school, but that since we were there the men would have to put up with us. His banter brought forth loud laughter from the male students. I was too humiliated to respond." Pauli Murray got the best revenge: she worked her way to the head of the class.

Murray's success at Howard did not provide her with a golden

Pauli Murray, later an eloquent advocate for civil rights for black Americans, was president of her class at Howard University Law School but still encountered sex discrimination there.

key to the future, however. She faced discrimination once again, this time at an elite white institution, Harvard. She was denied the opportunity to continue her legal studies there, not because of her race, but again because of her sex. Instead she went to the University of California at Berkeley, where she completed her law degree. Later, she wrote an important paper that influenced a landmark 1954 Supreme Court decision, *Brown* v. *Board of Education of Topeka, Kansas,* which ruled that the "separate but equal" provisions that justified segregated schooling was unconstitutional.

Pauli Murray was an exceptional woman, of course, and few women black or white achieved the kind of distinction and influence she achieved. Nevertheless, her story is typical of the drive and determination showed by African-American women in their struggle to achieve education, influence, and a better life for themselves and their children. Although they faced the double burdens of racism and sexism, often compounded by poverty, they were at the same time largely spared what Betty Friedan would later call the "feminine mystique," the trap of domesticity that constrained the lives of educated white women in the suburbs.

For white, middle-class women, college was an entry into affluent domesticity. Many must have believed that if they found a suitable mate at college, it made good sense to quit school and marry. By 1956, one fourth of all urban, white college women married while still in college. To do otherwise was a gamble. A woman who decided to postpone marriage, complete her education, and try to pursue a career during these years was likely to find it difficult, if not impossible, to gain access to a professional school or to find a job in the occupation of her choice. She might also find her chances for marriage reduced if she waited too long.

College-educated women often faced frustration when they tried to develop careers in their chosen fields. A survey of five thousand women who graduated from college between 1946 and 1949 found that two thirds had married within three to six years after graduation. Only half of these women had been able to find the kind of work they had wanted and for which they had been prepared. Those who had chosen occupations that were traditional for women, such as teaching, nursing, or secretarial work, were largely successful in finding positions. But fewer than half who sought work in science,

psychology, music, business, or journalism were able to find jobs. Many of these women ended up as secretaries, clerks, or receptionists. It is not surprising that these professionally educated women were often dissatisfied with their jobs.

The difficulty of developing a career no doubt encouraged many women to marry during college. Most universities were forced to discontinue their policies against married students and provide places for young couples to live. These arrangements made it easier for women to drop out of school and work or have children while their husbands remained enrolled. Young men and women were both advised that marriage during college was a good idea. Women were warned that their "chances for marriage are greatly reduced if they do not make a permanent attachment during the college years." Men were also encouraged to marry while in school. As one writer in the *Ladies Home Journal* advised, "Many young men find that they can do much better work if they get the girl out of their dreams and into their kitchens."

Vocational guidebooks and counselors urged women to use their

Training for the steno pool: young women in Minnesota master the fine points of the manual typewriter.

A class in food preparation at Iowa State University. Home economics took hold as an academic discipline, training women for future domestic responsibilities.

college education to prepare themselves to be well-educated house-wives, with some skills to fall back on in case of an emergency. This may have been realistic advice, given the limited employment op-portunities for women. Nevertheless, it caused many college-edu-cated women to resent their education for raising their expectations. They felt frustrated and bored because their desire for intellectual and creative work, which had been sparked in college, was unful-filled. This led many female graduates to call for changes in the col-lege curriculum that would be more suited to their jobs as home-makers. One female graduate later recalled, "An appalling number of graduates apparently felt that they should be more adequately prepared for their 'roles as wives and mothers' and suggested courses and reading lists to that end. I was horrified."

Older women watched the marriage mania among college stu-dents with alarm. Two such women who worked in a campus office tried to warn these younger women against early marriage. But they were unsuccessful. They were, one reported,

> characterized as bitter, unromantic old witches, in an affection-
> ate kind of way ... because we were anti-early marriage. We're
> both quite satisfactorily married, and I have two boys—it's only
> in recent years that I've had to go through the ridiculous business
> of explaining that I love them, that they "come first" even though

I've always worked at some kind of other job.... We did try to explain that we weren't unromantic—that was the funniest part, because our whole objection to this all-exclusive domesticity on the campus was that *it* was unromantic! Settling down, boy and girl in the library, making out lists of toasters, washing machines, towels. It seemed to us about the most unromantic thing we could think of, but we never got it across, and settled for being witches.

Dissenting voices were futile against the trend to tailor women's education toward domestic tasks. In 1949, Lynn White, president of Mills College, complained that "women are educated to be successful men. Then they must start all over again to be successful women." The domestic-oriented education that White and others fashioned at the time prompted a critical response from professional women, but it would be decades before feminists in great numbers would protest, as a representative of the National Organization for Women did in 1973: "What the universities are offering is an education designed to turn out efficient little suburban housewives with minor marketable skill so they can enrich their children's lives and not disgrace themselves in front of husband's business associates."

The effort to educate women for domesticity did have a number of advantages for women who would become career homemakers. It helped to professionalize the responsibilities of full-time wives and mothers, and to provide their work with dignity and stature. Improving the lot of the housewife was one way to push against the limits of domesticity. But in the long run, college curricula geared to the profession of homemaking did not solve the problems of frustration and boredom many educated women experienced. One explained her feelings this way: "This problem of the 'educated woman' learning to accept the monotony of housework and child training with cheerfulness and happiness has plagued me. I find much greater happiness now that the children are older," and she felt free to take a job outside the home.

Other housewives were more content. Some found that devoting themselves fully to the tasks of homemaking gave them a deep sense of satisfaction. They looked upon marriage and motherhood not as bliss, but as a challenging career with numerous rewards. One woman, who had seen her share of troubles as the wife of an alcoholic, made the best of it and focused on the positive. She took pride in her "husband and child and the chance to make a home for

A 1944 *advertisement suggests that purchasing war bonds will not only help the war effort but help women buy modern appliances to free them from kitchen chores. It also offers a booklet,* "Your Wedding Ring on the Window Sill."

The Women's Council of St. Paul, Minnesota, one of many service organizations in which black and white women joined to serve common goals.

them.... I always wanted marriage more than a career, and I have found the community activities one gets involved in (PTA, Girl Scouts, League of Women Voters, Women's Club, Church), keep you just as busy as a job and are equally stimulating." Although women were excluded from virtually all the positions of power in politics and business, many such career homemakers made an impact on local communities through their involvement in neighborhood voluntary associations.

Those were acceptable activities for women because they did not disrupt power relations in the home, and they fit prevailing attitudes about proper activities for women. Some women, however, pushed the limits too far, as far as their husbands were concerned. One young man found romance with a fellow student at college. "We are both studious and like to study the same things together," he wrote of his future wife. But later, that relationship turned sour. "My wife is a 'scholar,'" he complained, "has won her M.A. since marriage and is now working on her Ph.D. in addition to teaching mornings. I feel she spends too much time outside [the] home because our 4 children are all under 11—yet she is miserable when confined to home activity with only social activity outside the home." He believed that his wife was "too independent" and had "too much ambition."

A postwar tug-of-war: serving as Girl Scout leaders was one of the ways that suburban mothers made raising their children a full-time career.

In the face of this kind of opposition, some women gave up their aspirations. One such wife was resigned to her situation. She worked outside the home to help provide for the family, but she abandoned the career she might have pursued. "Frankly, I don't brood over the condition. . . . I'm never sorry for myself, just a little worried there is so little time left. And have I done what I wanted? I've always liked acting (had a few successful years in an amateur group in Hartford), but I couldn't be a mother, run a house, act, and go to work, so I gave up the theater. Now my pleasure is taking my daughter to plays and she seems quite interested. What is to be gained by lamenting what might have been?"

Women faced choices and trade-offs, and for many, life as a homemaker was preferable to the struggles associated with careers for women at a time when opportunities were so limited. One career homemaker claimed that she sacrificed nothing: "I gained and gained. [My husband] gave me things I longed for. Social position, nice family, background, the kind of home I wanted, money. . ." As a career woman, these trappings of the good life would have been nearly impossible to achieve. So this woman, like so many others, opted to marry and settle in the suburbs.

CHAPTER 5

SUBURBIA: THE HOMEMAKER'S WORK PLACE

I n 1959, the same year that the sheltered honeymooners were featured in *Life* magazine, Vice President Richard Nixon traveled to Moscow for the opening of a U.S. trade exhibition there. Nixon spent two full days debating with the Soviet premier, Nikita Khrushchev. Oddly enough, these two world leaders did not argue over who had better bombs, missiles, rockets, or even forms of government. Rather, they quibbled over who had better washing machines, televisions, and other gadgets. In what became known as the "kitchen debate," the two world leaders ultimately argued over who had better *women*.

Nixon boasted that "our goal is to make life better for our housewives," whose burdens were eased by appliances that would allow them to be attractive wives and attentive mothers. Khrushchev claimed that he did not share Nixon's "capitalist view of women," and instead took pride in the productive women workers who filled Soviet factories. Although neither side triumphed in the skirmish, the debate reveals an important fact about the Cold War era: families, homes, and consumer goods—along with the proper roles of women— had become high-stake political issues.

The locale of the appliance-laden American home, complete with perky housewife, was the suburb. Suburban developments sprang up all over the country in the wake of World War II. As developers

The geometry of the street plan of Levittown, New York, one of the first communities of tract housing built after World War II, symbolized the social conformity of the period.

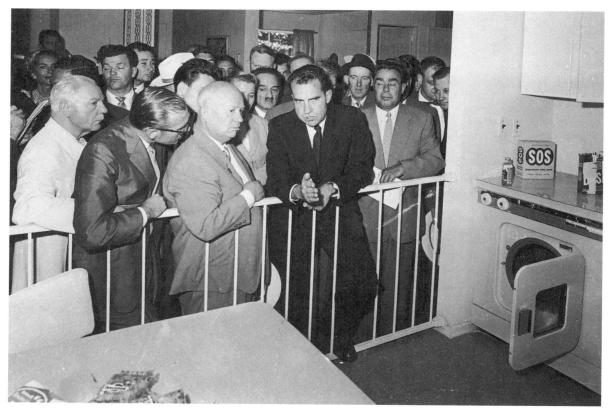

Vice President Richard Nixon (right) and Soviet premier Nikita Khrushchev (center) debate the relative merits of their countries' household technology at the American exhibition at a Soviet trade fair in 1959.

rushed to meet the postwar demand for housing, banks, government subsidies, and private investors poured funds into new, single-family homes. In 1946, for the first time, a majority of the nation's families lived in homes they owned. Over the next 15 years, 12 million more families became homeowners. These new houses in expanding suburban areas were built with young nuclear families in mind. Builders and architects assumed that men would be away at work during the day and houses would be occupied by mothers and children.

Most houses were designed with open floor plans where children could wander freely and safely. Kitchens usually opened into family rooms, with windows facing backyards, so that women could do household chores while watching their children. Living rooms featured picture windows, also to make it easy to keep an eye on children. The one-story design gave the home an informal look and was practical for families with small children, since there were no stairs, which could be dangerous. Houses were built with plenty of closet space to hold the numerous consumer goods that went along with suburban living.

Families did not have to be wealthy to buy houses in the suburbs. But they did have to be white. Racial minorities were not allowed to purchase homes in the suburbs, even if they could afford them. William Levitt pioneered in the development of standardized, inexpensive, mass-produced suburban homes available to white families of modest means. In the first Levittown, on Long Island, outside New York City, 17,400 houses accommodated eighty-two thousand residents. The structures were all basically alike, but they had flexible interior spaces that were easy to expand if the family increased in size. As young parents moved into these homes with their rapidly growing families, it is no wonder that the first Levittown quickly earned the nicknames "Fertility Valley" and "The Rabbit Hutch."

These homes were not particularly fancy or elegant, but they were filled with household appliances, the so-called "labor-saving" devices that would, presumably, lighten the housewife's burden. According to Vice President Nixon in Moscow, it was these labor-saving appliances that made it possible for housewives to be leisured and glamorous, not household drudges. Capitalism, according to American Cold War beliefs, made it possible for American women to keep their good looks, spend more time with their children, and be fresh and smiling when their husbands came home after a hard day at work. Appliances were not intended to give women more free time to develop hobbies, careers, or other interests. Rather, they enabled housewives to achieve a higher standard of cleanliness and efficiency, while allowing more time for child care. Housework could be more professional.

It is not at all clear that "labor-saving appliances" actually saved housewives any time. But it did make it possible for them to maintain an immaculate house. Women who were full-time homemakers spent as much time on housework as their mothers had, in spite of new appliances. The new gadgets, as well as new standards for cleanliness and order, may have actually added time. If it took less time to produce food and clothing, it took more time to shop. More time was devoted to family care as well. Cleaning took just as many hours, although it took less physical labor.

Laundry is a good example of this change. In the 1920s, many

The living room and exterior of a Cape Cod–style house in Levittown. The floor plans of most houses were identical, but in later years many owners made changes and additions.

A Sears Roebuck store in Syracuse, New York, proudly featured a washing machine, one of many appliances advertised to make women's domestic chores less burdensome.

houses lacked running water. Washing and ironing was heavy, time-consuming work. Laundry became much easier with washers and dryers. Yet, the amount of time spent doing laundry actually increased. People acquired more clothes and washed them more often, so the time for the chore expanded. Time spent on child care also increased. Best-selling baby-care books like the one by Dr. Benjamin Spock became household bibles that encouraged mothers to pay attention to their child's every whimper.

Consumer spending also increased the housewife's tasks. Shopping, driving, and selecting goods from the array of choices available became a major part of the household manager's routine. All together, full-time homemakers, like their mothers before them, still worked about 55 hours a week. Labor-saving appliances actually saved time only for women who worked outside the home. Employed women spent only about 26 hours a week doing housework. But, of course, that was in addition to the hours they spent at their paid jobs. Employed or not, care of the home and family remained women's responsibility. Ironically, the husband's place of rest was the wife's place of labor.

The home was also the center of family leisure. Postwar Americans spent a good deal of their incomes on items that would make the home comfortable and enjoyable: appliances, automobiles, backyard barbecue sets, and of course, televisions. By the 1950s, televisions were selling at a rate of more than 5 million a year. In their living rooms, ordinary families watched idealized families in enormously popular shows such as "Ozzie and Harriet," "Leave It to Beaver," and "Father Knows Best." These television families all had certain features in common: they were white, they lived in comfortable suburban homes, full-time homemakers had down-home wisdom and patience, and fathers always knew best. Curiously, although the fathers in these programs were the breadwinners of the family, we rarely if ever saw them at work. They were home, presiding with kindly, fatherly authority, clearly the head of the household. Nevertheless, mothers were the ones in charge of the daily routines, the running of the home, and the supervision of the children.

Television shows that featured working-class families were often continuations of radio comedy shows from the pre-TV era. Shows like "The Honeymooners," starring Jackie Gleason, depicted work-

ing-class men with real jobs (usually undesirable ones like bus drivers or sewer workers), wives who tolerated their husbands' explosive tempers and rolled their eyes at men's foolishness, and neighbors who shared their struggles. There were no children in these families, typically, but the couples were often preoccupied with purchasing consumer goods. They usually lived in apartments, rather than single-family houses, marking their distance from the child-centered suburban families featured in the middle-class situation comedies.

A few shows focused on ethnic Americans. "I Love Lucy," starring a Cuban band leader and his American real-life wife, made television history when the couple's child was born on the show before a TV audience of millions. "Amos 'n' Andy" featured black Americans who, despite moments of wit, wisdom, and shrewd cleverness, were depicted in stereotyped ways as clumsy bumblers. Television shows of the 1950s reinforced prevailing attitudes about white sub-

Promotional photographs for television, which became common in American homes by the late 1940s, showed the new device as a well-designed piece of furniture that would become the center of family life in prosperous households.

A suburban father passes on to his young son the traditionally male skills of lawn care.

urban families, working-class couples, and ethnic minorities. Nevertheless, these shows also brought Americans together around familiar characters and their daily struggles, making them somewhat more human than their stereotypes would suggest.

It is no wonder that television, the central consumer item in the American home, featured stories of American families and their consumer dreams. The ability to purchase these goods marked success in America, the American dream itself. Suburban Americans spent their money on their homes and on items that would enhance family life. Rather than spending money on personal luxury items such as furs and jewels, they were more likely to purchase appliances, recreational items, and cars. The suburban home became a self-contained universe. Family members would not even need to go out to have fun, since they had swing sets, playrooms, backyards, barbecues, and televisions right at home. Although critics have pointed with disdain at the drab conformity of suburban tract houses, these homes offered comfort at a modest cost. Most residents of Levittown claimed to be satisfied with their living arrangements.

Nevertheless, there were frustrations. The suburban ideal often promised more than it delivered. Obviously, appliances alone would not make a housewife happy. Women in Levittown often complained about feeling trapped and isolated, facing endless chores and tending to children. For them, suburban life was not a life of fun and leisure but of exhausting work and loneliness. Time-consuming commuting reduced the amount of time men could spend with their families, and for the suburban women who held jobs outside the home, the burden was even heavier. They faced work on the job, a long commute home, and then all the chores considered to be "woman's work" in the home.

The struggle to achieve the ideal suburban life took its toll on men as well as women. Since the primary goal of the "breadwinner" was to provide for his family, it was expected that he would work for the best steady pay, regardless of whether he enjoyed the job. The reward was in the quality of life that the man's income could buy—not the intrinsic satisfactions of the job itself. The woman's part of the bargain was to keep the home cheerful and clean, and to be content with the homemaker role. If either partner believed that the other was not keeping the bargain, trouble brewed.

The suburbs served as "bedroom communities" from which workers, mostly men, commuted to office jobs in the cities.

One housewife felt that her husband reneged on his side of the deal. "We were married during the depression years on a shoestring," she wrote,

> my husband lost his job soon after, and went into business for himself, also with no capital. Though he was excellent in his field (photography), he didn't have the drive necessary to sell himself, and we had very meager living for several years, til he got a factory job during the war. Though he did well, he liked having his own independence, and after quitting at several factory jobs because he didn't like the unfairness or domination, he started another business with a partner, in aerial photography. Then a series of unfortunate setbacks began ... eviction ... hurricane damage to his place ... injuries ... now my husband is back working for another aerial concern, but he dislikes the work, feels he is too old to start at the bottom in another line, and therefore is inwardly upset a good deal of the time.... I have always felt that he shouldn't cater to his feelings of having to be independent, and that he should take any kind of a good job with a steady pay... which would give us all a much stronger feeling of security.

This woman's words show how difficult the bargain became when a man's desire for independence and job satisfaction conflicted with his role as provider of a steady income. The marriage lasted until 1961, when they finally divorced. The only hope for material security came from the husband's income. If a wife held a job, her income would help but it would not pay the bills. And she would still

A mother carpools a troop of Boy Scouts in her Jeep station wagon. Many 1950s mothers made child care and related activities a full-time career.

be responsible for taking care of the home.

There were other potential problems with the expectation that the husband would be the sole or primary provider. Since the reward for his effort, and the mark of his success, took the form of consumer goods, the quest for consumer products could become obsessive. An affluent housewife explained the problem in what she considered to be her successful marriage:

> One fortunate thing which is important in our marriage is our fortunate change in income bracket. When we were married my husband earned $30 a week. We rented a five-room flat ... had a baby, etc. Now we have five children and an income of over $25,000 a year. We own our 8-room house—also a nice house on a lake. We have a sailboat, a Cris Craft, several small boats. We own our own riding horse which we keep at home. Our oldest child goes to a prep school. We have a Hammond organ in our home. ... Our two sons at home own expensive instruments. We have and carry a lot of life insurance. Unless some disaster hits us, we see our way clear to educate all our children thru [sic] prep-school and college.

All the goods this homemaker mentioned as marks of her family's success were geared toward home, family leisure, recreation, and education. She did not mention diamonds, mink coats, or other personal luxuries. Yet her pride in her shopping-list definition of marital success was tempered by a devastating comment she added, almost as an afterthought: "My reaction to all this is that my husband doesn't seem content to save. He continually seeks something new to own; he doesn't keep his interest in any one thing very long. He has terrific drive and aggressiveness, and I feel he tries to own all of us in the family too much." In this overblown case of domestic purchasing, even the wife and children became possessions to reflect the success of the male breadwinner.

If husbands had to work hard and sacrifice in order to earn enough to support the suburban way of life, women at home worked equally hard. In fact, there was no guarantee that affluence lessened their work load. The family's wealth did not provide this wife with much leisure, nor many opportunities to develop her own interests. Even community volunteer work was difficult. As one suburban housewife noted,

> Because of the size of our family, we have very little personal fun—I mean no clubs or activities. I used to be very active in PTA, church (taught Sunday school), and garden club, but my last two children now 4 and 2 years old changed all this. I just stay home with them and taxi my oldest boys around. Our oldest boy, almost 15, is away at prep school, but in our rural community I have to drive someone somewhere every day. I expect to get back into community life when my younger children are in school all day. I feel quite stale as though I don't use my mind enough.

Still, she felt satisfied with her life, in spite of a "stale" mind and an "overbearing inconsiderate" husband. She had worked hard to achieve the family life they had built on his income and her labor, and she was proud of her efforts.

For white, heterosexual, affluent, married women with children, suburban life had its rewards. It also had its drawbacks—some of them quite serious. These women knew that they had few alternatives for a satisfying and materially comfortable life, and if they wanted to have children their prospects for combining careers and motherhood were even slimmer, although a few managed to do it. But most turned their career aspirations to the home, and struggled to make homemaking a challenging, professionalized, satisfying life. Some were happier than others, but nearly all tried to make the best of the situation.

What about the women who did not have the resources to live the life of the suburban housewife? What about those whose ethnic or racial background, income level, marital status, or sexual orientation excluded them from these communities of nuclear families? For these women, like their white suburban sisters, there were hardships as well as rewards. Oddly enough, being excluded from the world of suburbia also gave these women a certain amount of freedom from its rigid expectations.

African-American women were not likely to avoid full-time domestic work. The difference was, they were more likely to do it in someone else's home. Bernice McCannon, for example, was a 30-year-old black woman who worked on an army base during the war, but fully expected to work again as a maid after the war. "I have always done domestic work for families. When war came, I made the same move many domestics did. I took a higher paying job in a government cafeteria as a junior baker.... If domestic work offers a good living, I see no reason why most of us will not return to our old jobs." Then she added, knowing what her options were likely to be, "We will have no alternative."

By 1950, 41 percent of all employed black women worked in

Domestic service, particularly caring for white children, remained a way of life for black women in both the South and North.

private homes. Another 19 percent worked in office buildings, restaurants, and hotels as scrubwomen, maids, and housekeepers. Of the remaining 40 percent, many worked in farm labor. In spite of the migration to the North, as late as 1950, 68 percent of African Americans still lived in the South. The lives of southern black women largely resembled that of their female ancestors during slavery: living in shacks, working sun up to sun down, forced to obey local white people or risk severe consequences.

In the North, as whites continued to move to the suburbs, blacks became more concentrated in the cities. By 1960 blacks were more urbanized than whites. North as well as South, black men earned less than half of what white men earned, and black women received less than half the amount that white women earned. Black women continued to face the most dismal prospects for paid employment, but they continued to take whatever jobs they could get.

In the postwar years, white women faced pressure to become full-time homemakers, and were often stigmatized if they held jobs. But black women faced no such stigma. Because of economic necessity, African-American women had a long history of combining paid work with domestic responsibilities. One advantage employed black women had over their white counterparts was that wage-earning African-American women commanded a great deal of respect within

Black women in the rural South, like this cotton picker in Alabama, endured a hardscrabble existence as sharecroppers on white-owned land.

Blacks in the North congregated in neighborhoods such as New York's Harlem, where they built lively communities despite economic hardship.

their communities.

White mainstream journals idealized the stay-at-home wife and mother and sanctioned employment only as an economic necessity. *Life* heaped disdain upon feminists of an earlier era:

> Unlike the strident suffragettes [campaigners for votes for women] who were once eager to prove their equality with men, the typical working wife of 1953 works for the double pay check that makes it possible to buy a TV set, a car—or in many cases simply to make ends meet. The problems created by her efforts to solve this are what happens to the children and what happens to her marriage. But most working wives, who have no intention of working indefinitely, feel it necessary to risk these dangers and cope with the problems in order to maintain a good standard of living for their families.

In contrast, the black press presented working wives and mothers in a heroic light. Rather than condemning the political agitators of earlier days, the African-American community connected black women's work with the struggle for racial as well as gender equality dating back to the 19th century. *Ebony* offered a tribute to "Women Leaders" in 1949:

> Their contribution to a fuller, richer life in the American tradition has been two-fold: they have aided in no small way the general fight of Negroes for integration in a living democracy and they have battled against the traditional enforced inferiority to the U.S. male.... Today's stout-hearted women who stand at the head of the onward march appropriately look back with pride to the glowing traditions handed down by such sterling heroines as Harriet Tubman and Sojourner Truth, who never accepted the myth that women belong to a weaker sex.

While *Ebony* praised black women with jobs, it also recognized that few black women had the luxury to be full-time homemakers. Poverty and discrimination filled the lives of black women with constant struggle. Some black families were fortunate enough to take advantage of postwar prosperity and allow mothers to stay home. For these women, homemaking represented a double triumph. As *Ebony* noted, "The cooking over which the 'white folks' used to go into ecstasies is now reserved for her own family and they really appreciate it."

At a time when white women were admonished not to compete against their husbands and to direct their career aspirations into the

home, black women were encouraged to pursue all opportunities. *Ebony* featured a "Medical Family," Jane and Barbara Wright, sisters who were each physicians married to lawyers. Another article featured "husband and wife teams" of prominent dual-career couples. While whites were warned that such arrangements would lead to neglected children and marital conflict, *Ebony* told its readers that "each couple is daily proving joint interests and twin careers to be both profitable and stimulating."

Of course, the families featured in *Ebony* were no more typical of black Americans than the notables featured in the white press were typical of white Americans. But the magazine did reflect a different set of values. Those values extended not only to the wealthy black families featured in the news, but to the majority of black Americans who faced financial hardships. Although these African-American families were deprived of the material benefits available to white Americans, they were also spared some of the drawbacks of life in the suburbs.

Suburbs fostered tightly knit nuclear families in loosely knit communities and extended family networks. People moved often, and

Black schoolteachers enjoyed great respect in their communities. They symbolized the goal of African-American parents for their children to get a good education and rise above jobs in the service economy.

ties to neighbors were often weak, since the nuclear family was expected to be self-sufficient and self-enclosed. People did come together in a number of associations, most notably in the churches and synagogues that sprang up across the country. The suburban landscape was dotted with religious institutions, as Americans joined congregations in record numbers. People also came together in local civic institutions. Women joined local PTAs, women's clubs, and charities, and they organized scout troops and other enrichment programs for their children.

These efforts provided women with community ties, and gave them the opportunity to shape social, religious and educational institutions in their neighborhoods. These were important tasks. But deep sources of mutual support and tight networks based on kinship and friendship were difficult to achieve in the suburbs. People moved in and out too quickly, and many left their relatives and ethnic communities when they moved to the suburbs. The isolation of the nuclear family also inhibited the casual visiting that took place on the stoops of urban apartments or the streets of the cities.

Those outside the suburbs were more likely to develop strong ties of support with relatives and friends. It was both more possible, and more necessary, to do so. Take, for example, the Jacksons, an African-American family from rural Arkansas. Most blacks still lived in the rural South, in spite of the massive migration northward that began early in the century, increased substantially during the war, and continued steadily in the postwar years. In the half century between the mid-teens and the '60s, 96 members of the Jackson family joined that migration and moved North. First they moved to rural areas in the North where they worked on farms. Eventually they settled in cities. Wherever they settled, they clustered with their relatives. While white suburban family arrangements centered around the married couple and their children, this was not necessarily the typical family formation for African-American migrants to northern cities. Often the strongest ties over time were among siblings.

Siblings often left the South together or followed one another. Sometimes they lived together or near each other with spouses or children, providing mutual aid such as cooking and child care. In 1945, for example, Caroline Jackson left her husband and daughter in the South with her parents and moved to Wisconsin to harvest

fruit. At the same time, her brother's wife died, leaving him with two young sons. He decided to move north and join Caroline in Wisconsin, where he got a job in a catsup factory. He and Caroline lived in trailers next to each other. Caroline cooked for them all and cared for the children. They lived this way for a year and a half before returning to the South, where they rejoined the rest of their families.

Family attendance at church services and other religious activities was a focus of suburban life for many Americans. For those who had recently moved from ethnic neighborhoods, churches and synagogues provided new social communities.

Poverty and discrimination made it extremely difficult for poor African-American women to live according to the suburban ideal. The inability to find adequate jobs broke up many families. Caroline Jackson lived apart from her husband in order to gain better employment opportunities. Even the welfare system often separated families; for a woman to get welfare, she could not be living with a man. In the postwar years, 25 percent of African-American wives were either separated, widowed, or divorced, compared to 10 percent of white women.

Ruby Lee Daniels struggled against heavy odds to build a secure life for herself and her children. An illegitimate daughter of Mississippi sharecroppers, she came north after the war and moved into an apartment with her aunt. The janitorial job she got at Montgomery Ward paid her four times as much as she had earned as a waitress in Mississippi. But the North was not paradise. She still struggled against poverty. She married young and separated quickly, had two children, and never settled down with a man. Her real family were her female friends and relatives, who helped her find shelter and work, and helped her raise her children. She hoped she would find a good man, a good job, and a home of her own in Chicago. But her dream never came true. For Ruby Lee Daniels, poverty and the difficulties of being a single mother prevented her from achieving her goal.

The family strategies of Ruby Lee Daniels and Caroline Jackson, based on strong ties of kinship, functioned well for African Americans who were excluded by poverty as well as racism from white suburban America. But as long as American society was deeply racist, segregation had some advantages for African Americans. It protected them and their children from constant degradation and harassment in their daily lives. As Carolyn Reed recalled of her childhood

Urban blacks, like this charwoman cleaning a Greyhound bus in Pittsburgh, commonly found employment in menial, low-paying jobs.

Some blacks in the Northern cities achieved economic success. Black-owned businesses like this dress shop in Chicago catered to the middle-class African-American community.

in a segregated neighborhood, "Teachers then ... were marvelous—black teachers that were really interested in helping children." She remembers one of her teachers telling her, "You are as good as anyone—you're just as good as anyone, but you're not better than anyone." It is not likely that a white teacher in the early 1950s would have been so encouraging to a young black girl. As we shall see, these strong community supports served them well when African Americans came together in the most powerful grass-roots political movement of the century: the civil rights movement.

American women in the postwar years, whether white and middle class living in the suburbs, or black and poor living in the rural South or inner cities, struggled mightily to push against the limits set by rigid racial and gender boundaries. They carved out meaningful lives as best they could, while the institutions in which they lived and worked tried to keep them "in their place." In spite of the conservatism and conformity of the era, women continued to expand their horizons and opportunities where they could, in their work lives, in their homes, in their communities, and in their most intimate relationships as well.

SEX:
DATING, MATING, AND
THE DOUBLE STANDARD

World War II was over and the wartime anxieties about single women out in the world of men seemed to have subsided. American men and women rushed into marriage and retreated into the safety of their own bedrooms. But peacetime did not bring sexual tranquility. Rather, the sexual terrain remained a minefield. Until very recently, sexual restraint was a time-honored moral code in America. Men were usually forgiven their sexual indulgences; it was almost expected that young men would "sow their wild oats" before marriage. But women were not allowed such indulgence. They were expected to be virgins when they married. By the middle of the 20th century, however, women began to explore their sexuality in new ways, often outside marriage. Although sexual activity among young women was by no means uncommon, it still carried severe consequences. The "double standard" that allowed men more sexual freedom than women was still in full force. But as they had tested other restraints, women pushed against the sexual boundaries, too.

Maria K. and Betty M., participants in a 1955 study of marriage and family life, explained how costly it was to push against the boundaries of the sexual double standard. According to Maria K.,

> The freedom of our relations before marriage saved us many stresses and strains we might otherwise have had. On the whole, how-

Undergraduates pair off at the student union of the University of Minnesota. College offered many opportunities for young people to find marriage partners.

Social life was lively on university campuses as men and women prepared for their futures as breadwinning husbands and homemaking wives.

ever, I would say it was unfortunate. Despite his failure to recognize it then—or now, for that matter—I have concluded that my husband has deep emotional conventionality such that the attitudes our "free love" experience fostered undermined his respect and admiration for me. This is pure guesswork—but I think we established a set of "mistress patterns" that had far reaching unhealthy effects for our marital adjustment. Also it was stupid of me not to anticipate that his oft-expressed philosophy of the desirability of sexual freedom indicated that he would be prone to infidelity. I didn't expect it, and it came as a severe blow. An even worse blow was his amazement at this, and his statement that faith in a partner's constancy is sheer stupidity. I have been faithful, but doubt if he believes this.

Maria K. paid dearly for the premarital sexual intercourse she enjoyed with her future husband. Betty M. did too, but for her the cost was different:

Our courtship did not result in marriage for over six years for educational and financial reasons. Our engagement had no definite beginning but was taken for granted after perhaps a year or two. Complete sexual experience therefore developed gradually and naturally after two or three years. (Without the moral codes of our civilization to which I tried to be loyal, it would have happened much earlier.) I feel this gradual introduction to sex experience has advantages over being plunged into it suddenly on the wedding night. However, it carried with it for me a high sense of guilt which still bothers me after all these years. I am forever grateful that we did finally marry because I probably would never have felt free to marry anyone else. This feeling of guilt may be why I am unable to respond sexually as I wish I could. I am glad I never indulged in petting with anyone but my husband.

The experiences of these two women suggest the power of post-war taboos against premarital sex. Maria K. and her fiancé freely broke the rules. Yet Maria would suffer for her transgression for years to come. In the eyes of her husband, she became morally suspect, even though they both willingly participated in their premarital sexual activity. She believed that his lingering suspicion of her provided him with justification for his own adulterous behavior later, ultimately poisoning their marriage. Betty M., who became sexually active within a stable, long-term engagement, was nevertheless so tormented by her own guilt that she was never fully able to enjoy sex with her husband.

Sex and reproduction affected women's lives much more powerfully than men's. The mid-century decades were particularly treacherous ones because the codes of sexual conduct were changing so rapidly. On the one hand, traditional sexual mores and the "double standard" remained so strong that a woman's reputation could be "ruined"—in the lingo of the day—if she behaved in ways that were outside the boundaries of acceptable sexual conduct for women. If she became pregnant as a result, the consequences were extremely dire.

On the other hand, these were the years when sex became big business; sex was used to sell products from cars to toothpaste. It was also a time when sex came to define the cornerstone of marital happiness. Magazines, movies, and every form of advice literature encouraged women to be attractive and sexy to catch a man—but to put on the brakes when it came to sex itself. Birth control devices were becoming more effective and available, but abortion remained illegal except under exceptional circumstances, and illegal abortions were extremely dangerous. If women were confused by all these mixed

Images of attractive women helped companies sell products as mundane as Pepsi-Cola.

messages, it is no wonder. As one woman recalled, "Postwar America was a society with Stop-Go lights flashing everywhere we looked. Sex, its magic spell everywhere, was accompanied by the stern warning: Don't do it."

The American sex ethic, like the work ethic, seemed to define central beliefs about the national culture. But when Alfred Kinsey published his now-famous studies of American sex life, *Sexual Behavior in the Human Male,* in 1948, and *Sexual Behavior in the Human Female* in 1953, the nation and the world learned that Americans did not practice what they preached when it came to sex. Kinsey, an unassuming zoologist, wrote these two massive tomes that documented, in hundreds of pages of facts, figures, and tables, American sexual habits. Although these scientific texts were incredibly dry and boring to read, they instantly became best-sellers, so eager were Americans to read about their own private behavior.

Kinsey found that nearly all men engaged in masturbation and heterosexual petting, and that almost 90 percent had premarital intercourse. Half admitted to having extramarital sex, and more than a third had homosexual experience. For women, the numbers were not quite so high, but equally surprising to a society that still believed in female chastity. More than three fifths of the women had engaged in masturbation, 90 percent had experienced petting, half had engaged in sexual intercourse prior to marriage, and a quarter in extramarital sex. These statistics indicate the extent to which Americans violated their own codes of conduct. Kinsey's studies revealed what American men and women *did*—but not how they felt about it. It is in the feelings that went along with the actions—love, anger, guilt, resentment, disappointment, and satisfaction—that the full story of postwar sexuality needs to be understood.

The behavior Kinsey documented went far beyond what was considered appropriate, even at a time when expectations about sexual conduct were changing. These were years of "sexual liberalism," which meant that some physical expressions of affection, such as petting, were sanctioned. Even intercourse did not carry the stigma it once had, particularly if the couple were in love and planning to marry. But as the cases above reveal, traditional beliefs about proper sexual conduct were held so deeply that they might still affect people's feelings and relationships through their entire lives.

One of the most surprising findings in Kinsey's study was the extent of homosexual activity among Americans. The war and postwar years opened up new possibilities for gay men and lesbians to socialize and form relationships. During the war, the armed services provided places for same-sex relationships to develop, far removed from the scrutiny of family and neighbors. Pat Bond, a wartime teenager who enlisted in the Women's Army Corps, feared that her attraction for women would condemn her to be "forever alone." But when she joined the service, she found a pleasant surprise. "Everybody was going with someone or had a crush on someone," she recalled. "Always the straight women I ran into tended to ignore us, tended to say, 'Who cares? It leaves all the men for us.'" Another woman who joined the navy fell into a relationship with another recruit whom she "admired greatly." She explained, "We didn't talk about what

Dr. Alfred Kinsey conducts an interview for his classic report on Sexual Behavior in the Human Female. *Men and women shared the most personal details of their sex lives with Dr. Kinsey.*

we were doing, we just did it and felt good about it. I just thought, 'Well, this is the way it's going to be forever.'"

Civilians also found new ways to meet partners in the wartime social scene in the cities. One young lesbian was amazed at the boldness she encountered when she moved to Los Angeles to find work and lived in a boarding house for single women. She had no idea how to find other lesbians until she overheard a conversation among her neighbors. "I thought, 'Gee, I wonder if these are some of the girls I would very dearly love to meet' . . . I started talking and finally they asked me, 'Do you like boys, or do you go out strictly with girls?'" Her new friends introduced her to other lesbians and showed her around the lesbian bars that were springing up in Los Angeles. These ties, forged in wartime, continued in the postwar years as the network of lesbian communities grew and flourished.

Phillis Abry, a lesbian, enlisted in the army and served in a radio repair unit. She was based at South Plains Army Air Field in Lubbock, Texas.

Gay bars were centers of social life for homosexual men and lesbians. But the bar scene did not appeal to all lesbians. Other networks also served the social needs of lesbians, including business and professional women's organizations and friendship networks. A woman doctor recalled the "wonderful parties where we could be ourselves. . . . It gave me an identity, a self-identity and for the first time a community identity."

Kinsey had revealed that "persons with homosexual history are to be found in every age group, in every social level, in every conceivable occupation, in cities and on farms, and in the most remote areas of the country. . . . In large city communities . . . an experienced observer may identify hundreds of persons in a day whose homosexual interests are certain." It was now obvious that homosexuality, once considered a deviant fringe element of society, was pervasive. But in the hostile climate of the Cold War years, this knowledge did little to make life easier for gay men and lesbians. In fact, the postwar era was a time of heightened persecution of homosexuals.

Anyone who did not display the appropriate sexual behavior of the era—heterosexual dating, young marriage, and childbearing—was suspected of being a "pervert." This pejorative term was widely used during these years and implied not only sexual deviance, but danger. The Republican party national chairman, Guy Gabrielson, claimed that "sexual perverts . . . have infiltrated our Government in recent years," and they were "perhaps as dangerous as the actual Communists." It was widely believed that only "manly" men could stand up against the threat of communism, and that "perverts" were security risks. The persecution of homosexual men and women became more intense than ever before.

Homophobia became ferocious, destroying careers, encouraging harassment, and forcing homosexuals to name others with whom they associated. In 1950, the Senate issued a report on the *Employment of Homosexuals and Other Sex Perverts in Government,* which asserted that "those who engage in overt acts of perversion lack the emotional stability of normal persons. . . . Indulgence in acts of sex perversion weakens the moral fibre of the individual." Male homosexuals were considered the greatest menace. Lesbians were also condemned, but since displays of affection between women were

Lesbians gather for a night out at a Buffalo, New York "gay girls" bar during the war. Some sported "butch" haircuts and men's clothing.

not uncommon, lesbianism more easily went unnoticed.

Nevertheless, lesbians established strong communities with distinctive styles of dress, behavior, and social institutions. Lesbians who were open about their identity faced extreme hostility and even violence. The lesbian community in Buffalo, New York, for example, established a number of local bars in the downtown area. The public bar community gave the Buffalo lesbians a strong feeling of solidarity and support as they confronted a hostile outside world. These women faced a constant struggle to maintain their dignity. In the postwar years, when male and female roles were sharply distinguished in dress and behavior, similar distinctions developed in the lesbian community. "Butch" lesbians usually wore their hair short and dressed in styles that resembled men's clothing, while their "femme" partners wore an exaggerated feminine style. One lesbian recalled, "There was a great difference in looks between a lesbian and her girl. You had to take a streetcar—very few people had cars. And people would stare and such."

By the 1950s, these lesbians faced violent attacks. One later recalled that she struggled against persecution to make life easier for younger lesbians who would follow: "Things back then were horrible, and I think that because I fought like a man to survive I made it somehow easier for the kids coming out today. I did all their fighting for them.... I left them a better place to come out into.... But I wouldn't deny it; even though I was getting my brains beaten up I would never stand up and say, 'No, don't hit me, I'm not gay, I'm not gay.' I would not do that." The strength of the community gave women like this the courage to face such violent hostility.

Lesbianism was the most flagrant violation of the sexual code for women, but there were many types of violations. Nonmarital sexual behavior of any kind was problematic for women. There was, of course, one easy way for young women to avoid the difficulty altogether: get married. Even some lesbians used marriage as a cover for their sexuality. But the solution was much easier for young heterosexual women. In the postwar years, teenage sex was considered bad only if the teenagers were unmarried. It is quite possible that one reason the age at marriage dropped so precipitously during these years was that youngsters married in order to engage in sex legitimately. Although the rate of *premarital* intercourse did not rise significantly during these years, the rate of *teenage* sexual intercourse rose dramatically. The reason: these teenagers were married.

At the same time, marriage itself was sexualized in new ways. Followers of the psychoanalyst Sigmund Freud popularized his ideas that sexual repression was unhealthy. People should enjoy sex—but only in marriage. In fact, good marriage depended upon good sex, according to many experts at the time. A professor of education at Whittier College warned that if married partners were not sexually satisfied, their children would suffer: "Children need happily married parents.... When there are lacks in the sharing of satisfaction in sexual relations, some sort of deep and fundamental disappointment occurs. Each partner goes his way feeling unfulfilled and thwarted, and both find themselves incomprehensibly irritable and tense in situations which the child has a part.... The matter, then, of sexual adjustment between the parents was found to be related to children's difficulties and maladjustments to a very important degree." He concluded with a statement that summarized much of the thinking of the era: "Wholesome sex relations are the cornerstone of marriage."

But experts continued to contradict themselves and give confusing advice. If sex was so important to marriage, then sexual attraction should play a major role in choosing a spouse. At the same time, young people were warned against putting too much emphasis on sexual attraction. One expert proposed a scientific formula for mate selection: "60 percent profound affection and respect [and] 40 percent intense sex attraction." With this balance, "you can be fairly sure that you'll get the happy, fantastic, fairy-tale result." Unfortunately, he claimed that most marriages were based on 70 percent sexual attraction and 30 percent genuine affection, a formula likely to lead to divorce.

All experts agreed, however, on the importance of sexual compatibility in marriage. But they gave no hints as to how that compatibility would be determined prior to marriage. As one wife recalled after many years of marriage, "Looking back on it, I do not believe I gave the matter [of sex] anywhere nearly enough thought or consideration. Appreciating, as I do now, the importance of a normal, satisfying sexual relationship between husband and wife, I marvel at my good fortune in being lucky enough to have married a man who *is* suited to me, sexually, and vice versa. On further thought, I don't really know how I would have gone about finding out, had I been concerned." Most couples were expected to engage in a limited amount of sexual intimacy before marriage, stopping short of intercourse. This restraint was supposed to lead to sexual ecstacy in marriage—but that did not necessarily happen. Most women who engaged in premarital intercourse did so with their future spouse, and often the marriage followed soon after. Sometimes the guilt resulting from sexual intercourse prompted a couple to marry quickly.

The path to marriage was expected to start during high school, and young women were to take charge of the matter. The key was allure. Magazines aimed at young girls were filled with tips on "how to catch a husband" or "how to snare a male." But this catching and snaring was supposed to happen passively: never "give the man the idea you are running after him; pretend to let him catch you." Much of the skill of man-catching involved subordinating the girl's thoughts and feelings to those of her date—good practice for a marriage in which the man was expected to be the head of the household. "Concentrate on your companion's feelings instead of your own ... learn to talk about things that interest men," young women were told. The important thing was to "arouse and hold a man's interest."

Dating began the path to marriage. Most young people dated during high school, and many, especially young working-class women

The formal wedding was the most important rite of passage for young adults in the 1950s. This happy couple would soon move to the suburbs, where they raised their daughter.

who did not go on to college, married right after graduation. The dating system established a certain amount of physical intimacy between unmarried men and women. Although the proportion of young men and women having sexual intercourse did not increase substantially between the 1920s and the 1960s, there was a significant increase in physical intimacy that stopped short of intercourse. As Kinsey noted, on "doorsteps and on street corners, and on high school and

Dating patterns typically began early, as at this high school dance in Minnesota. Teenagers were encouraged to begin the process of mate selection early.

college campuses, [petting] may be observed in the daytime as well as in the evening hours." He claimed that petting was "one of the most significant factors in the sexual lives of high school and college males and females."

Dating and petting in high school often encouraged young coupling, and those who were steady dates were more likely to become sexually involved. One teenager explained that it had more to do with love than with sexual experimentation: "Something you go all the way in should only be with someone you really love, not just any date." Although adults at the time were sometimes alarmed at what they saw as promiscuous behavior, dating and petting, and even intercourse between steadies, was part of a system of dating that was expected to lead, ultimately, to the rational choice of a marriage partner.

The dating and petting system, however, contained many dangers for women. It was very difficult for a young woman to know how to avoid being a "prude," and at the same to know how far was "too far" to go and still maintain her reputation and desirability. The "double standard" was fiercely enforced, which meant that boys could experiment sexually with little risk, but girls were condemned if they did so. It was a confusing and stressful situation for young women. Boys were expected to try to go as far as possible with the girls they dated, and girls were expected to set the limits.

Young women who gave in to the pressure often paid a very high price, by losing the boy's affection or her reputation, or, in the worst case, becoming pregnant. Said one pregnant 16-year-old, "How are you supposed to know what they want? You hold out for a long time and then when you do give in to them and give your body they laugh at you afterwards and say they'd never marry a slut, and that they didn't love you but were just testing because they only plan to marry a virgin and wanted to see if you'd go all the way." One episode like this was enough to mark a "good girl" as a "bad girl" and destroy her reputation.

"Good girls" did not have sex. Or, if they did, it was only with someone they truly loved. But to complicate matters even more, the situation was exactly the reverse for young men. If men dated young women they "respected" and truly cared for, they would not have sex with them. As one male college student explained, "I felt that if I were sexual with someone, that indicated that I didn't respect them. I could be sexual with someone I didn't care for, but not with someone I did care for. The fact that I was never sexual with anyone is because I never dated anyone I didn't care for."

This strange logic permeated social relations between young men and women, causing tensions and confusions constantly. Social class played a role in these sexual maneuvers. One youth felt it was "all right for a boy to go as far as he wants, but not with the girl he is to marry or with a girl in his own class." These divisions were present in both the white and black communities. One young southern black man said, "There are some that I run around with and can do anything to, and there are some who won't let you mess with them. I don't mess with girls I go with because they are nice girls, and I don't believe it's nice to bother nice girls."

Young women struggled to assert their own desires for intimacy, affection, and sexual exploration within the complicated rules of the double standard. Many bent or broke the rules, or claimed their rights to their own desires in the rapidly changing sexual climate of

Social life at women's colleges such as Radcliffe was formal: the women entertained male callers at tea, and there were strict rules regulating male visitors to students' rooms.

the era. Gradually they chipped away at the more brutal aspects of the double standard. As one study at the time concluded, "Values have probably changed ... at least to the extent that more girls accept premarital coitus *if* there is an emotional involvement with the partner and some commitment by him to marriage in the future."

But even sex with a steady boyfriend, or a fiancé, was fraught with potential consequences unforeseen at the time. Sometimes the commitment to marriage came after the fact. As one woman recalled of her decision to marry her husband, "The fact that we had been intimate, I am certain, made my mind set for marriage to him." Apparently, it was not a good enough reason, for she later regretted her "poor choice of mate" and divorced him. Another woman confessed that even after marriage, she feared that her reputation would be ruined if people knew they had engaged in premarital sex: "I was afraid that someone might have learned that we had intercourse before marriage and I'd be disgraced."

These comments indicate the terrible strain a woman was under to be sexy enough to catch her man, but not too sexy to lose him. Women suffered the stigma of "promiscuity," and risked the danger of pregnancy. They had to walk the difficult tightrope between sexual allure and the emphasis on virginity that permeated the youth culture. Kinsey found that half of the men he interviewed wanted to marry a virgin—although it does not appear that he asked the same question of women (whether *they* wanted to marry a virgin). Kinsey understood that this pressure to remain sexually chaste might lead to guilt and psychological disorders: "Behavior which is accepted by the culture does not generate psychologic conflicts in the individual or unmanageable social problems. The same behavior, censored, condemned, tabooed, or criminally punished in the next culture, may generate guilt and neurotic disturbances in the nonconforming individual and serious conflict within the social organism." Kinsey's anthropological language described postwar America quite accurately. For women, whose bodies would bear the reproductive consequences of sexual activity, the matter was complicated indeed.

Here's a man your wife should know

(If you own a Plymouth, Dodge, De Soto, Chrysler or Imperial)

She (and you) should get to know him very well because *he knows your car.* He's the MoPar man in your community—your "Forward Look" car dealer or leading independent serviceman.

His specialty is *keeping* you *proud* . . . keeping your car looking and operating like a million.

And in doing that he saves you money, because

1. His staff is trained and experienced in the particular requirements of *your* car . . . knows what to do and how to do it.

2. He's the man with MoPar products—*genuine* Chrysler Corporation parts and accessories, engineered precisely with your car in mind.

3. He's equipped with special factory designed and approved tools to save service time and lower labor costs.

Your MoPar man is the kind of businessman you like to do business with, too. He knows that he can't succeed *tomorrow* without giving you the best in service *today.*

genuine, Chrysler-engineered

**MoPar Division, Chrysler Motors Corporation
Detroit 31, Michigan**

Advertisements betrayed a sexual double standard, using a slightly suggestive headline to sell auto parts while expecting women to uphold high moral standards.

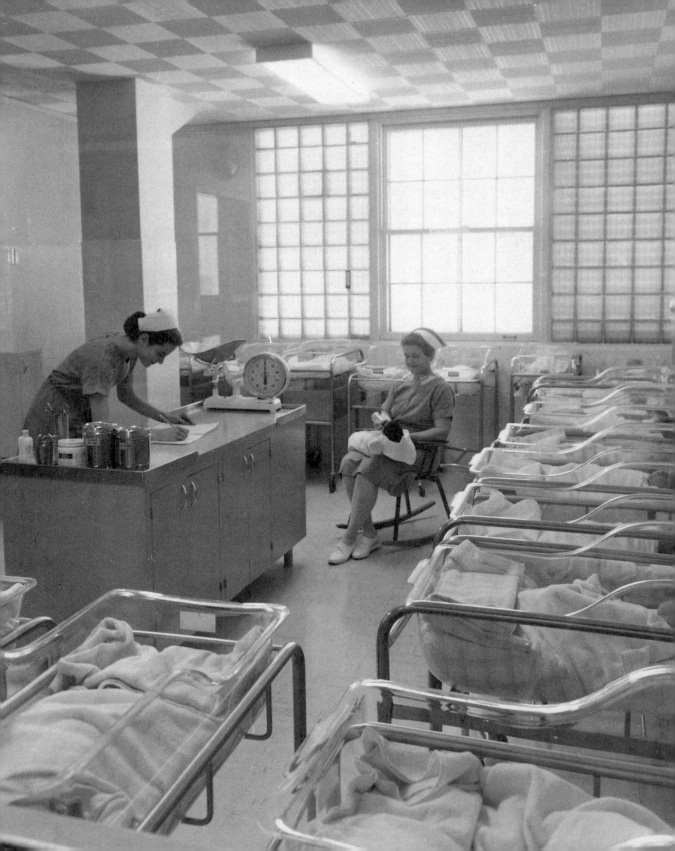

CHAPTER 7

REPRODUCTION: BIRTH CONTROL, ABORTION, AND THE BABY BOOM

F or all the confusion and tension surrounding sex outside of marriage, sex was supposed to blossom in marriage. Safely expressed within the home, sex could lead to its ultimate purpose: reproduction. Experts at the time claimed that the fullest expression of a woman's sexuality was motherhood. In 1947, Ferdinand Lundberg and Marynia F. Farnham, two Freudian psychologists, wrote a best-selling book about women's sexuality, *The Modern Woman: The Lost Sex*. They argued that the goal of female sexuality is "receptivity and passiveness, a willingness to accept dependence without fear or resentment, with a deep inwardness and readiness for the final goal of sexual life—impregnation."

Women who did not accept this idea, according to Lundberg and Farnham, "constitute the array of the sick, unhappy, neurotic, wholly or partly incapable of dealing with life.... They have always been known and simply recognized for what they are—the miserable, half-satisfied, the frustrated, the angered." Much of their scorn was heaped on feminists of an earlier day. With absolutely no evidence, "experts" such as these claimed that feminists, "when they came to perform the sexual act, found that they were frigid." But mothers were sexy.

This was a new idea. Previously, motherhood had been associated with chastity and purity. But the new sexy vision of mother-

A full hospital nursery, the ultimate symbol of the Baby Boom. After a century and a half of steady decline, the birthrate rose dramatically in the 1940s and 1950s.

Fifties mothers were expected to remain beautiful and sexually attractive even while supervising the outdoor activities of their children.

hood appeared as early as 1944, when *Life* featured an article on "Model Mothers," professional models who had babies. The article began, "Here are family poses of some professional beauties who have found that having a baby is fine for their careers ... having babies is no hindrance to the careers of the professional models who make a good living displaying their pretty faces and fine figures for photographers and illustrators. Motherhood, in fact, seems to help them.... Being a mother usually improves a girl's disposition, her attitude towards her work, her looks and even her figure."

The very meaning of marriage began to be identified with having children, and women were expected to achieve their greatest fulfillment in motherhood. Given the strong connections among female sexuality, marriage, and motherhood, one might expect that the birth control movement would have withered during these years. On the contrary, the movement gained momentum.

Under the leadership of Margaret Sanger, birth control had gained a great deal of support among political liberals during the 1920s and 1930s. In those years, it was associated with women's rights. After birth control became legal under federal law in the 1930s, the number of birth control clinics in the nation grew rapidly, from 55 in 1930 to more than 800 in 1942. In that year, the Birth Control Federation of America changed its name to the Planned Parenthood Federation of America, signaling a major shift in the movement's philosophy. New goals focused not so much on the rights of women to control their own reproduction, but on strengthening the family through liberating female sexuality in marriage. If women did not fear pregnancy, they would be more likely to enjoy sex with their husbands, leading to happier families.

In addition, birth control made it possible to postpone and space children, so that families could be scientifically and rationally planned. During the 1950s, there was rapid progress in birth control technology. Condoms, diaphragms, jellies, and foams were widely available. Research moved ahead on the intrauterine device (IUD) and on oral contraceptives. "The Pill," as the birth control pill came to be known, was approved by the Food and Drug Administration in 1960.

Birth control was not to be used by unmarried women to prevent pregnancy, nor by married women to avoid motherhood. Rather, it was another scientific advance to enhance family life. Like washing machines or vacuum cleaners, birth control devices might be considered "labor-saving appliances" that would make a homemaker's job as wife and mother happier, easier, and more scientific.

Of course, the widespread use of birth control did not result in a declining birthrate. Rather, it may have actually contributed to the Baby Boom by enabling couples to marry young and have the number of children they wanted. When women were asked what they thought was the "ideal" number of children, the most common response went from two in 1940 to four in 1960. Women were marrying and having children younger than their grandmothers had. Most had their children while they were in their 20s, and they used birth control to postpone and space their children as well as to prevent further pregnancies after they had completed their families.

By 1961, the National Council of Churches of Christ had approved the use of birth control devices. Nonorthodox Protestant and Jewish organizations moved from outright hostility to enthusiastic approval, even making it a moral obligation to control family size. The medical profession agreed. At the same time, state legisla-

Margaret Sanger, shown here at the opening of a birth control clinic in Tucson, Arizona, in 1953. She had been an active crusader for contraception and women's rights since the 1920s.

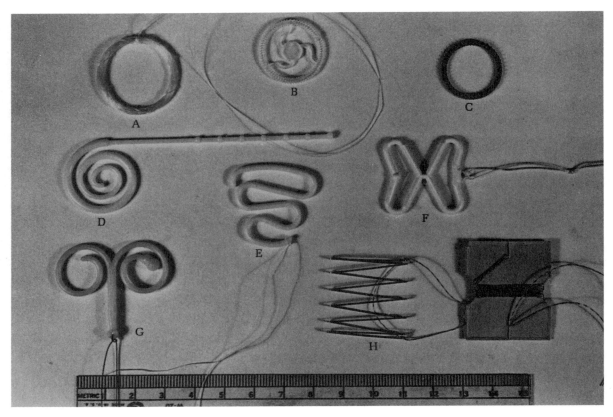

The 1950s saw considerable progress in the development of intrauterine devices (IUDs) made of stainless steel, plastic, and other synthetic materials. The goal was to improve their effectiveness as birth control devices and to minimize infections.

tures were loosening their restrictions on birth control. Before the war, most states banned the distribution of contraceptive information and materials, even to doctors. But most of these restrictions were eliminated by the 1950s. Now birth control was considered a means of strengthening families.

Increased availability and the removal of legal restrictions led to widespread use of contraceptives among married couples. During the 1950s, 81 percent of white wives of childbearing age used birth control. White middle-class Protestant couples were the most likely to use birth control, and contraceptive use among other groups was increasing. American society was ready to accept birth control as a means to improving marital sex and family planning. But it was not ready to accept its potential for liberating female sexuality outside of marriage. American public opinion, lawmakers, and physicians all did their part to make sure that birth control would encourage marriage and family life. Consequently, one of the most explosive scientific developments of the postwar years, which held the promise of freeing sex from marriage and marriage from procreation, did neither. That potential was not realized for two decades.

Advocates of family planning endorsed contraception but drew the line at abortion. While birth control was promoted as a means to strengthen families, abortion was considered a threat to sexual morality and family life. If birth control was the reward for the virtuous, abortion was the punishment for the immoral. The American Social Hygiene Association warned that illicit sex could lead to the abortionist's door, and illustrated the point in its pamphlet with a picture of a frightened-looking woman walking up a dingy stairway in an obvious slum. Illegal abortions were indeed dangerous, but the association urged sexual restraint rather than legalized abortion.

Legal abortions had been available for several decades, but they became more difficult to obtain in the 1940s and 1950s. Legal abortions could be performed only if physicians decided that continuing the pregnancy would present a danger to the woman's life or health. In most states, physicians were able to interpret the danger as they saw fit, and some women were able to obtain safe, legal abortions in hospitals. But in the postwar years, physicians and hospital boards became increasingly reluctant to approve legal abortions, sending thousands of pregnant women into the back alleys to have dangerous operations performed illegally.

In spite of the risks, abortions were still quite common. There were an estimated 250,000 to 1 million illegal abortions each year during these decades, which were responsible for about 40 percent of all deaths of pregnant women. Among the women surveyed in the Kinsey report in 1953, one in four of all wives said they had abortions by the time they were 40, and nearly 90 percent of premarital pregnancies were aborted. Educated black women were as likely to obtain abortions as educated white women; those with less education were more likely to carry their pregnancies to term. Most abortions were illegal.

There were probably fewer abortions performed after the war than before, due in part, no doubt, to the increasing availability of birth control. Nevertheless, sensational articles in the popular press about illegal "abortion rings" (illegal businesses) increased. This media attention to the subject of abortion warned young women of

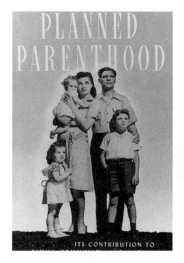

Literature distributed by Planned Parenthood promoted not just birth control but a broader concept of well-planned families that would strengthen communities and the nation.

the dangers of illicit sex. Horrific as these stories of botched abortions were, desperate women continued to terminate unwanted pregnancies.

Illegal abortions were a last resort. Joyce Johnson was 28 years old when she sought an abortion in New York in 1956. As she gave the abortionist $500, her ordeal began:

> "Leave on the shoes!" he barked as I climbed up on his table almost fully clothed. Was I expected to make a run for it if the police rang his doorbell in the middle of the operation? He yelled at me to do this and do that, and it sent him into a rage that my legs were shaking, so how could he do what he had to do? But if I didn't want him to do it, that was all right with him. I said I wanted him to do it. I was crying.... The whole thing took two hours, but it seemed much longer through the pain.... He gave me pills when it was over, and told me I could call him only if anything went wrong. "But don't ever let me catch you back here again, young lady!" I staggered down the cement steps of his house with my life.

Another young woman, who was married, had a more sympathetic abortionist. She left a family gathering a few days after an abortion because she was running a fever and hemorrhaging. When she arrived by taxi at the abortionist's house,

> She let me in and I was crying and I was feverish. There was a little table there and she put me on it.... She started working on me and I was crying and she came and I will remember this till the day I die, she came and put her arms around me on the table like that, and she said, "Honey, did you think it was so easy to be a woman?" Given the humiliations and hazards, it is testimony to the determination of these women to gain control over their reproduction that so many took these risks.

For unmarried women unable or unwilling to have an abortion, having a baby out of wedlock presented enormous difficulties. As with so many aspects of postwar life, the experience of unmarried pregnancy differed greatly for white and black women. Sally B. was white; Brenda J. was black. Both were 16 years old when they got pregnant in 1957. Both girls' parents were upset by the news. But from that point on, their stories diverged. Sally's parents owned a dry cleaning store in a city in Pennsylvania. When she told them she was pregnant, they were horrified. They were furious at Sally and her boyfriend, Tim, whom they had forbidden her to date. To make matters worse, as soon as she told Tim she was pregnant, he lost interest in her. Sally hardly knew where to turn.

Her father, who had done business in the community for 20 years, was very concerned about what their neighbors would think about the disgrace Sally had brought upon her family. He suggested that they send Sally away, and tell their neighbors and friends that she was dead. But Sally's mother offered a different solution. They would tell the school that Sally had been invited to spend spring semester with relatives in San Diego. Then they would send Sally to the Florence Crittenton home for unwed mothers in Philadelphia, where she would stay until the baby was born. Until the time that Sally left, she stayed at home with her angry parents, who refused to let her leave the house. In a few weeks, before Sally began to look pregnant, she was whisked off to the home for unwed mothers.

At the Crittenton home Sally was hidden from public view. She and other girls, most of them white, who had "gotten into trouble" took classes in grooming, sewing, charm, and cooking. Sally told the social worker that she wanted to keep her baby. But the social worker claimed that it was not normal for an unmarried girl to want to keep her baby. She said that Sally was suffering from a number of psychological disorders that caused her to think that she wanted to keep the baby. The social worker met with Sally every week, and by the time her baby was born she had been persuaded to give the baby up for adoption. She had been convinced that she had done something so wrong that she did not deserve to keep her child. "I don't think any unmarried girl has the right to keep her baby. I don't think it's fair to the child. I know I don't have the right," said Sally sadly, after her baby girl was born. The child was adopted by a Philadelphia lawyer and his wife who were infertile. Sally was back home before her 17th birthday. Her social worker and her parents warned her severely to keep the entire episode secret for the rest of her life, and to pretend that it never happened.

Brenda J. had a very different experience. Brenda lived in New York with her mother, a sister, and two brothers. Brenda did not have to tell anyone about her pregnancy—her mother figured it out when Brenda was about two months along. Brenda's mother was upset. She was unhappy about Brenda leaving school, and disgusted

Florence Crittenton homes like this one in Philadelphia provided a haven for unwed mothers. Young women spent their pregnancies safe from public embarrassment but under the watchful eye of social workers.

that Brenda was thinking of marrying the baby's father, her 19-year-old boyfriend. She convinced Brenda to give up that foolish idea: "It's better to be an unwed mother than an unhappy bride. You'll never be able to point your finger at me and say, 'If it hadn't been for her.'" Brenda stayed in school until she was expelled by the dean of girls.

Brenda's boyfriend continued to spend time with Brenda, but as she got bigger she was sure he was going out with other girls too. After she was expelled from school, Brenda ran errands and helped her mother, who worked as a maid for a middle-class family. As the time for her delivery drew near, she began to worry about how she would take care of the baby. Her family had no extra money and no extra space for a baby. Brenda considered giving up the baby, perhaps to relatives in South Carolina. But her mother told her, "You put your child away, you might as well kill him. He'll think no one wants him."

When Brenda's baby was born in the local public hospital, Brenda told the nurse, "I love the baby as much as if I was married." Brenda had no money, and her boyfriend left to find work in Florida. So Brenda went to the welfare office, where she was sternly lectured about girls having sex and taxpayers paying the price. She was told that she had to find the baby's father if she wanted welfare, and that the welfare people would be watching her apartment.

The stories of these two girls describe the dire consequences for young women who got pregnant out of wedlock. Typically, white girls were shrouded in secrecy, banished from their homes and families, and virtually forced to give up their babies for adoption. These girls provided babies for the adoption industry, since infertile white couples during the Baby Boom years were desperate to find healthy white infants. Black girls, on the other hand, were more likely to stay in their families and be encouraged to keep their babies. Most homes for unwed mothers did not accept non-white clients, and the demand for black babies to adopt was not as great as for white babies.

For black and white teenagers, marriage was one solution. If a white girl became pregnant, the father of her child might be forced into a "shotgun" wedding by the girl's parents, but often these marriages did not last long. Other times, the couples decided to marry

The prime goal of sex education was to prevent young women from having babies out of wedlock. Young people were encouraged to date and mingle but to abstain from sexual intercourse until they got married.

sooner than they had planned, or perhaps the pregnancy made them decide to get married. In any case, with the marriage age dropping rapidly, marriage was one way to solve the problem of unwed pregnancy. For young white couples who had the resources to marry, marriage avoided the stigma of illegitimacy.

Young couples who could not afford to marry right away might postpone the wedding. One young African-American woman from the South had her baby and continued to live with her tenant-farmer parents. But her relationship with her fiancé was solid: "We was in love and just couldn't wait to get married [before having sex].... He's living out here in the country now, working with his papa ... I still loves Connie. He comes over to see me and treats me and the baby nice. We wants to get married soon's he can make a little more money." In this case, both families supported the young couple as they tried to get established; there was no "shotgun" wedding, and the boy did not reject his girlfriend as soon as she became pregnant. But not all young pregnant women were so fortunate.

The different treatment of black and white unwed mothers reflects how white and black women were regarded almost as sexual opposites. Since African Americans first arrived in this country, they have been treated as though they were sexually more "wild" and "primitive" than whites. This unproven assumption provided the basis for widespread rape of black slave women by their white owners, and the constant suspicion surrounding black men that led to countless lynchings. Myths of black female sexuality also promoted contrasting myths of white female purity. These myths victimized both black and white women: black women were routinely exploited sexually by whites, and white women were routinely denied the expression of their own sexual feelings.

The effects of these long-held beliefs about sex and race continued well into the 20th century, when they continued to affect young women coming of age. Sally and Brenda both found that once they got pregnant, they had few options. Their paths were determined largely by their race. And yet both girls grew up during a time when sexual attitudes, mores, and behavior were in flux. Neither girl was "promiscuous," a disparaging term frequently used during these years to condemn young women (but never young men). Both obviously had sex with their boyfriends out of feelings of love, even though both boys ultimately left them with full responsibility for the conse-

A nurse counsels clients on family planning at a birth control clinic founded by Margaret Sanger.

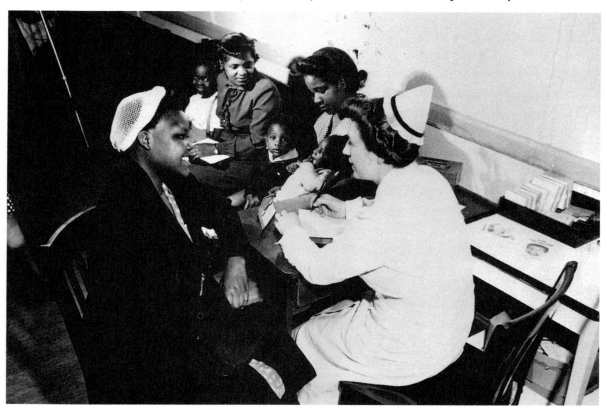

quences of their sexual relationships. Throughout these decades, women had to navigate the sexual minefield with great care—for they were at much greater risk of getting hurt than their male peers were.

Although black unwed mothers were more likely to keep their babies, and white women to give them up for adoption, both endured the stigma of unwed motherhood. A study of 50 unwed black mothers in Indiana in 1957 found that two out of three of the girls' families punished them severely, and that most of the girls described their babies as unwanted. Many had tried to get abortions, and when they were unsuccessful, they tried to have their babies adopted. Another study concluded, "Most mothers of children born out of wedlock expressed great feelings of guilt and were fully aware of the stigma in the Negro and general community."

Unwanted babies, of course, were not necessarily unloved. Many babies born to married parents were not planned or "wanted" until they arrived. Illegitimate babies may well have been loved, but they and their mothers faced a difficult life ahead. As a result, many pregnant girls felt that the best they could do for their children was to put them up for adoption. During the 1950s, some of the homes for unwed mothers began to provide services to black women as well as white, and some of the facilities became integrated. But few black women were able to take advantage of the opportunities available at the homes. White women suffered the trauma of unwed pregnancy, isolation, and the sadness of giving up a baby. But then they could put the whole episode behind them. Black women who had babies out of wedlock usually faced a long and difficult struggle to provide for themselves and their children.

Unwed pregnancy, like unwed sex, was condemned because it happened outside marriage. Inside marriage, however, both were celebrated. Married couples in the postwar years wanted large families. In one study of middle-class white couples in the mid-1950s, 39 percent wanted at least four children. As one wife recalled, "After the first baby, I wanted company for her and had a second daughter. A miscarriage left me with such a feeling of failure that I wanted the third child. The fourth was a happy accident. So now we're really 'happy' to be blessed with our two boys and two girls." For this woman, a miscarriage represented a "failure," even though she had no control over it. And an unplanned pregnancy was a "happy acci-

All the children get in on the act as their father consults with an agricultural adviser. Large families were the goal of many couples, in cities as well as on farms.

dent." Her story reflects the ways in which children were seen as blessings; large families were considered to be happy ones.

Of course, not all large families were happy. Children required care, attention, and money. The desire to provide college educations for all of their children was one reason why some parents limited the size of their families. As one mother explained, "I think if money had not been such a worrisome thing and if we had not had so many periods of unsteady jobs, we might have had more children." Another said, "After the first two were born and we appreciated the joys of parenthood it was mutually desired to have more children. We have stopped at four only because we feel the financial burden of educating more than four is more than we can see our way clear to assuming. We would both like six children. And it is not too late to change our minds about stopping at four!"

At a time when motherhood was supposed to provide fulfillment for women, few dared to complain about the stresses of childrearing. Women who chafed against the burdens of full-time motherhood were often accused of being selfish or "neurotic"—another common word at the time used much more frequently to describe the mental state of women than of men. One woman admitted that she believed there was more to life than constant child care. "The expenses of raising a child made us feel two would be enough. For we wanted to give a college education, music lessons, etc. to each child, if he showed interest. Also the interests I have had in church and community activities made me discontent with constant baby or child care." But comments like these were rare.

Why did postwar women and men want, and have, so many babies? There is no simple answer. The Baby Boom of the 1940s and '50s was accompanied by a widespread set of beliefs favoring large families. These ideas were found everywhere, from magazines and TV shows to medical advice. Public policies, such as tax breaks for parents with dependent children and financial support for suburban home ownership, encouraged couples to have children. Still, one needs to ask why postwar couples—especially women—wanted large families.

One explanation is that prosperity encouraged people to have babies. There is certainly some truth to this, but there were other prosperous eras that did not spark a Baby Boom. And one study concluded that the evidence provided no support at all for the idea that higher income caused a higher birthrate between 1940 and 1960. Nevertheless, numerous children, like numerous appliances in the home, symbolized abundance.

There are some cultural explanations. Many educated women made homemaking their career, investing it with skill, prestige, creativity, and importance. Considering how difficult it was for women to build professional careers outside the home, it is not surprising that many women poured their energies into their families. As the *Ladies Home Journal* put it, "Increasing numbers of women, disillusioned with their present roles or with what the workaday world can offer, will turn toward motherhood as the happiest road to fulfillment." But motherhood could be full time only as long as there were young children at home. Once the children entered school, motherhood could not be full time, unless the woman had more children. Having additional children could extend the years of one's chosen career as a full-time mother.

It is no wonder that women responded to Dr. Spock's call for professionalized childrearing and propelled his parenting guidebook to the top of the best-seller list. If the occupational achievement of a man was reflected in the income he brought home, a woman's achievement might be measured by the number of children she raised successfully. As one father expressed it in 1955, "I'd like six kids ... it just seems like a minimum production goal."

With so much emphasis on having babies, those who did not have children faced both pity and scorn. Women in particular suffered if they were unable to have children. Since motherhood was expected to be a woman's main source of satisfaction, many childless women said that they felt "abnormal" and "unnatural." The adoption industry flourished during these years, with most of the demand coming from infertile middle-class couples and most of the supply coming from unmarried white girls and women. At the same time, the treatment of infertility practice became a booming medical field, even though only half of all cases could be diagnosed and treated. Although it was well known at the time that infertility was as likely to result from a problem with the man as with the woman, treatment was usually focused on the woman. Some doctors went so far as to operate on healthy, fertile women before checking to see if the problem might reside with the husband. Many women suffered through the pain and humiliation of infertility treatment in their desperate efforts to become mothers and live out the expected role of postwar women.

A proud mother with her infant daughter in 1955. At right, the same glowing mother, who gave up her career as an economist to raise her daughter, helps celebrate her fifth birthday.

A happy homemaker supervises a cookie-baking session. For white middle-class women, sharing domestic pleasures with their daughters was a source of great personal fulfillment.

As with other aspects of life for American women, women pushed the limits of sexuality and reproduction as far as they could, given the constraints they faced. They struggled to maintain the fine line between sexual allure and sexual misbehavior, while redefining acceptable female sexuality before and during marriage. Those who fell outside the norm of acceptable conduct—single mothers, lesbians, and the childless—struggled to achieve lives of dignity. And those who produced and reared the Baby Boom children put their greatest energies into the task.

CHAPTER 8

PUBLIC LIFE:
GOING AGAINST THE GRAIN

While much of white America retreated to the suburbs; conformed to the consumer, corporate way of life; and avoided political activism at a time when anti-Communist crusaders could easily destroy the lives of political dissenters, black America was busy marshaling the most important grass-roots political movement of the century. The civil rights movement captured the attention of the nation in 1955 with the Montgomery, Alabama, bus boycott. It began when Rosa Parks, an African-American woman, refused to give up her seat to a white person on a bus. But the seeds of the civil rights movement had been sown over many decades. In the 1950s, the seeds bore fruit.

Rosa Parks became famous for her heroic act of defiance. But she had long been active in the struggle for equality. In December 1955, she and two other women, Jo Ann Robinson and Virginia Durr, took action to end the segregation of buses. All three women were born in the South. Parks and Robinson were granddaughters of slaves; Durr was the granddaughter of slaveholders. Durr had been educated at Wellesley College, a women's college in the North, where she first learned to live with blacks as equals. She later married and moved to Washington, D.C., where she worked for the Democratic Women's Committee while rearing four children. Durr

Both black and white women participated actively in demonstrations and sit-ins for civil rights. Their placards compared American racial policies to the apartheid of South Africa.

Rosa Parks takes her place at the front of the bus on the first day that Montgomery, Alabama, buses were integrated, December 21, 1956. A year earlier, she sparked a boycott of Montgomery buses when she refused to give up her seat to a white passenger.

worked energetically to abolish the poll tax, a device used mostly in the South to charge money for the privilege of voting, effectively denying the vote to many blacks, poor whites, and women.

The Durrs returned to the South after the anti-Communist hysteria led by Senator Joseph McCarthy became unbearable for them, and they became active in the National Association for the Advancement of Colored People (NAACP). There Virginia Durr met Rosa Parks, who was a seamstress at a local department store and secretary of the NAACP. The third woman, Jo Ann Robinson, was the 12th and youngest child of a farm family who owned their own farm in Georgia. She was the first in her family to attend college, and like most African-American women who began college, she graduated. She went on to earn a master's degree at the historically black Atlanta University, and in 1949 she joined the faculty of Alabama State College, another all-black institution, in Montgomery. She became active in her church, the Dexter Avenue Baptist Church, and also joined a black professional women's civic organization.

Robinson was not familiar with the system of segregation on the city buses. She owned her own car and drove wherever she needed to go. But one day she was going out of town and decided to take the bus to the airport. Without knowing that she was doing anything illegal, she sat down in one of the first 10 rows of the bus—those reserved for whites. She did not realize the bus driver was yelling at her until he stood over her shouting, "Get up from there! Get up from there!" with his hand up ready to hit her. In horror and humiliation, she ran from the bus. But the pain of that moment stayed with her, and she waited for the right opportunity to challenge the system.

Over the next several years, a number of black bus passengers refused to give up their seats. Each time, the black community wanted to take action, but they were not well enough organized. Finally, the time was right. On December 1, 1955, Rosa Parks left her job and caught the bus home. She sat in the black section of the bus, but the bus filled quickly and the driver demanded that she give up her seat to a white passenger. Technically, according to the law, blacks were not required to give up their seats if there were no other seats available further back in the bus. So Rosa Parks was in fact within her legal rights when she refused to move. Nevertheless, she was arrested and jailed.

Clifford Durr, Virginia Durr's husband and an attorney, bailed her out. Durr could easily have had the charges dismissed, because Parks had not violated the law. She was not required to give up her seat because there were no other seats on the bus. Parks's husband was terrified and wanted the charges dismissed. "Rosa, the white

The "Ease That Squeeze" poster was a commentary on the traffic in Montgomery, not the boycott by black residents. Despite traffic and the inconvenience of walking or carpooling to work, blacks remained steadfast in their boycott of the buses.

folks will kill you," he begged. But Rosa Parks and her friends were determined: they would not have the charges dismissed. They would use the case to test the constitutionality of the segregation system, known as the Jim Crow laws.

While Parks awaited trial, Jo Ann Robinson worked energetically with a few of her students to draft, duplicate, and distribute thousands of fliers urging blacks to stay off Montgomery's buses. Here the active network of organized women moved into high gear. They took batches of fliers all over the city, where members of the Women's Political Council distributed them. Four days after Rosa Parks's arrest, she was tried and convicted. On that day, no blacks rode the Montgomery buses.

Parks decided to appeal the decision, and the boycott continued. The night of the trial, more than ten thousand people gathered at Holt Church for a mass meeting. A young minister who had just moved to Montgomery, Reverend Martin Luther King, Jr., spoke passionately to the gathering, urging that the protest continue and calling for nonviolent resistance. From that moment on King was considered the leader of the nonviolent movement for civil rights. But women were powerful rank and file activists carrying the movement forward.

The participation of black women was most apparent in the bus boycott. Since they comprised the largest group of bus riders, their refusal to ride the buses made a huge dent in the revenue the buses needed to operate, making the boycott enormously successful. But these women sacrificed mightily to participate in the boycott. For an entire year they walked from their homes on one side of town to the homes of their white employers on the other. "My feet is tired, but my soul is rested," said one elderly African-American woman of her daily trek. They had to deal not only with tired feet, but with hostile white city leaders who tried desperately to break the boycott.

The efforts of these women, along with the strength of the networks and political alliances that kept the boycott going, yielded tremendous success. In 1956 the case finally went to the Supreme Court, which ruled in *Gayle* v. *Browder* that Montgomery's Jim Crow laws, which enforced strict racial segregation in public places such as buses, stores, and restaurants, were unconstitutional because they deprived blacks of the equal protection of the laws guaranteed by the 14th Amendment.

By now the civil rights movement was in full swing. Martin Luther King, Jr., and other African-American leaders formed the Southern Christian Leadership Conference, and they hired Ella Baker, head of the New York chapter of the NAACP, as administrative assistant. Although Baker was an experienced veteran of the struggle for civil rights, and was probably the best person for the job as director of the organization, she was given a subordinate position. Baker was resigned to the situation, and explained it this way: "As a woman, an older woman, in a group of ministers who are accustomed to having women largely as supporters, there was no place for me to come into a leadership role." But from her position behind King's limelight, Baker mobilized the movement.

Baker had grown up in the South and had graduated from the all-black Shaw College. But her college degree earned her jobs only as a waitress and factory worker. During the 1930s and the war years, she was an active organizer for civil rights. In 1954, when the

Prior to the Supreme Court's ruling in Brown v. Board of Education, *blacks were customarily educated in poorly equipped, segregated schools.*

Supreme Court decided the *Brown* v. *Board of Education* case, ruling that segregated schools were unconstitutional, she became president of the New York City branch of the NAACP and worked to integrate the city schools. Later, when she helped to found the Student Nonviolent Coordinating Committee (SNCC) in 1960, she encouraged young students to violate segregation statutes all over the South by sitting in at lunch counters and registering voters in areas of the Deep South where blacks had been prohibited from voting for more than half a century.

By the early '60s, the danger and violence faced by civil rights activists had escalated to terrifying levels. But the movement continued, and it began to attract young whites from the North as well as the South to join the struggle. During the early years of the civil rights movement, few whites were directly involved. Some watched from the sidelines, some provided moral and material support, and some fought aggressively against the protestors. There were a number of white churches whose leadership supported the cause of equal rights; there were others who were opposed. Women were on all sides of the issue. Some southern white women participated in the bus boycott by driving their maids to and from work, either in sympathy with the effort or simply because they needed their hired help. Others were hostile. A few, like Virginia Durr, were active participants. But by and large, white women, like white men, shunned political activism in the 1950s.

There were reasons, of course. For white Americans, trying to hang on to the fragile prosperity and security postwar life offered, political activism during the Cold War years was dangerous business. The mere suggestion of participation in any left-of-center politics could cost their jobs and reputations. Although participation in the civil rights movement was extremely dangerous, African Americans had a great deal to gain. They were willing to risk taunts, threats, beatings, intimidation, and even death. Whites had little to gain and perhaps much to lose by challenging the system. All across the nation, in Hollywood, on college and university campuses, in government offices, individuals suspected of left-wing sentiments were tarred with the brush of suspicion by the anti-Communist crusaders. Under the circumstances, it was difficult for whites to muster the courage to fight for the rights of African Americans. It was not until the

1960s that whites became active in the movement in significant numbers.

White women found other ways to influence public life, however. One way was through the voluntary organizations that emerged in cities, towns, and suburbs across the country. In churches, schools, charities, scout troops, and numerous civic clubs, women volunteered their time. Many middle-class women built virtual careers, and gained prominence and influence, through their volunteer efforts. As membership in churches and synagogues expanded, women were active in religious groups of all kinds, from choirs to Sunday schools to charities. In these groups, women learned new skills and forged networks that helped them overcome the isolation of their domestic routines.

For some, voluntarism was a direct route to power. Alice Leopold had been president of the League of Women Voters and director of a visiting nurses' program before becoming secretary of state in Connecticut in 1953. Because of her earlier experience as a volunteer, she knew how to get an equal-pay-for-women bill through the state assembly. In 1954 she organized a conference on the Equal Rights Amendment, and later in her career she became director of the Women's Bureau in the U.S. Department of Labor.

A few notable women held positions of power in the 1950s, and used their positions to challenge the outrageous conduct of Senator

Alice Leopold became director of the Women's Bureau of the U.S. Department of Labor in 1953. She proclaimed, "Women are becoming increasingly important in the development of our country's industry, in scientific research, in the education field, and in the social sciences."

Senator Margaret Chase Smith represented Maine in Congress from 1940 to 1973. She was a forceful advocate of Title VII of the Civil Rights Act of 1964, which banned discrimination on the basis of sex as well as race, creed, and national origin.

Joseph McCarthy, who from 1947 to 1954 led the anti-Communist crusade against people with liberal views. McCarthy and his followers accused many innocent people of being security risks, disloyal citizens, Communist sympathizers, or "perverts," destroying careers and lives as he went along. Senator Margaret Chase Smith from Maine was one of the few who called upon the country to resist "fear, ignorance, bigotry and smear."

Other women used different channels to raise their voices in protest. Women newspaper publishers such as Katherine Graham, Dorothy Schiff, Agnes Meyer, and Alicia Patterson took liberal stands on issues like civil rights and McCarthyism, as the anti-Communist hysteria came to be called. Author Lillian Smith wrote on behalf of women's rights and racial equality, in spite of hostile critics. Dorothy Day published the *Catholic Worker* newspaper and wrote often about poverty and peace issues.

Mary McCarthy (no relation to Joseph) wrote many essays defending liberals and assailed the loyalty oaths and conformity required by McCarthyism. She was horrified by the attacks on intellectuals and teachers. She claimed that American students were not in danger of indoctrination by Communists, but rather were in danger of "being stupefied by the complacent propaganda for democracy," which was "pious, priggish, and groupy."

Other women writers, including Lillian Hellman and Diana Trilling, opposed Senator McCarthy and spoke out courageously. Women scholars also registered their protest against life as it was. Rachel Carson, for instance, wrote a number of influential books calling for sensitivity to the environment, notably *The Sea Around Us* (1951), capping her career in the 1960s with her powerful warning about dangerous chemicals, *The Silent Spring*.

All across the country and in many different ways, individual women called for change and resisted the most oppressive conditions of the era. But these efforts represented a prelude to the major upheavals that would begin in the 1960s. Efforts on behalf of women's rights were not well organized during the '50s. There was a small group of older women who continued to work together during the postwar years. They had forged a strong alliance earlier in the century as part of the National Woman's Party. Although this small group of active feminists continued their efforts after the war, the momentum for women's rights collapsed.

Most of the active women's organizations in the postwar years were apolitical. Groups like the League of Women Voters, Business and Professional Women, and the American Association of University Women were white middle-class mainstream groups that worked in the public interest, but did little to challenge the system. Only a few associations, such as the YWCA, began to build new alliances across race and class that would bring women from different backgrounds together to forge a new agenda. A few women joined the "beat generation," a mostly male counterculture of artists, poets, and bohemians. Most of these women were in supportive roles to the men, but a few women made names for themselves as artists, notably abstract expressionist painters like Elaine de Kooning and Joan Mitchell. A few poets also emerged, notably Denise Levertov, Barbara Guest, Adrienne Rich, Anne Sexton, and Sylvia Plath.

In addition to these notable women, there were also signs of stirring evident beneath the surface of postwar complacency. While most women experienced discontent in isolation, as exhausted housewives or underpaid and exploited workers, a few groups did begin

The Don't You Wish You Knew Club in Minnesota. By the 1950s integrated community organizations were becoming more common.

Sylvia Plath reads in a poetry contest while a student at Smith College in the 1950s. She went on to write intensely personal poetry and prose. Her novel The Bell Jar *was published in 1963, the year she committed suicide.*

to organize on their own behalf. In 1950, for example, when Chicano miners in New Mexico went on strike to protest wage cuts and unsafe conditions at the Empire Zinc Company, women began to mobilize to change the conditions of their lives. They had long suffered under miserable living conditions in company-owned towns, where they lived in shacks with no running water. They were unable to work in the mines and had no other job opportunities, so they were totally dependent upon their husbands' earnings. During the strike, they began to ask why the striking men were not demanding better housing conditions.

The men dismissed the women's concerns as trivial. But soon the situation changed. Miners were forbidden to picket, and the company brought in truckloads of strikebreakers to take their jobs in the mines. Women suddenly took up the picket lines. Drawing upon the skills and friendships developed in their churches and neighborhoods, they bravely faced the police. Now the men, who had laughed at their domestic concerns, found themselves at home changing diapers and washing clothes—with no hot water. Women meanwhile found strength with each other on the picket lines, and in the crowded jails where they were thrown with their babies. Jailers hardly knew what to do with all the women who sang together even as their babies cried. When the women returned home, the men understood their needs, and they had gained new respect.

Another example of women's organizing emerged in the tiny lesbian community in San Francisco, where in 1955 a lesbian couple, Del Martin and Phyllis Lyon, founded the Daughters of Bilitis. They advocated equal rights for homosexuals and provided "a home for the Lesbian. She can come here to find help, friendship, acceptance and support. She can help others understand themselves, and can go out into the world to help the public understand her better."

Like the African-American women in the South who gave birth to the civil rights movement, the wives of the Chicano miners and the lesbians in San Francisco were already so excluded from mainstream American society that their struggles seemed worth the risks involved. They did not reap the benefits of the affluent society. They did not live on tidy, tree-lined suburban streets. They did not suffer from what Betty Friedan would later call the Feminine Mystique. Although the anti-Communist crusaders who followed in the path

of Senator Joseph McCarthy would consider these women un-American, they were simply asserting their claim as Americans, wanting to be included in the American dream, wanting their full rights as citizens.

But even for those who presumably lived the American dream, discontent was beginning to surface. In March 1960, *Newsweek* discussed the plight of the housewife: "All admit to being deeply frustrated at times by the lack of privacy, the physical burden, the routine of family life, the confinement of it. However, none would give up her home and family if she had the choice to make again." *Redbook* chimed in the same year, offering a $500 prize for the best account of "Why Young Mothers Feel Trapped." More than twenty-four thousand women responded.

By the early 1960s, white middle-class women were beginning to fight back. On November 1, 1961, fifty thousand American housewives walked out of their homes and jobs in a massive protest, "Women Strike for Peace." These activists were among the first postwar middle-class whites to organize against the militarism of the Cold War. Sev-

In the 1950s and 1960s, women took their place in the picket lines of organized labor: above, outside an auto parts plant in Detroit, and below, to protest discriminatory hiring practices in the retail and service industries.

eral of the leaders of the strike, including Dagmar Wilson, Eleanor Garst, Jeanne Bagby, and Margaret Russell, were part of the small group of women who had been active in the peace movement and other liberal causes during the '40s and '50s. But most of the strikers were ordinary young housewives. According to *Newsweek,* the strikers "were perfectly ordinary looking women.... They looked like the women you would see driving ranch wagons, or shopping at the village market, or attending PTA meetings ... many [were] wheeling baby buggies or strollers." Within a year their numbers grew to several hundred thousand.

Anti-Communist crusaders worried that Women Strike for Peace signaled that "the pro-Reds have moved in on our mothers and are using them for their own purposes." The Federal Bureau of Investigation (FBI) kept the group under surveillance. In 1962, the leaders of the group were called before the House Un-American Activities Committee (HUAC), a committee much feared and hated by political activists becuase of the way it had destroyed the lives and careers of hundreds of Americans during the worst years of anti-Communist hysteria. But with the Women Strike for Peace activists, the Committee met its match. The tables were turned and now the women taunted and humiliated the congressmen.

For three days, the committee hearing room was in turmoil. Hundreds of women packed the room, hissing, booing, shouting, applauding, and making no effort to quiet their noisy babies. The congressmen who tried to prove that these women were Communists looked ridiculous. The women were not intimidated and frightened the way most of the HUAC witnesses were. Retired schoolteacher Blanche Posner lectured the congressmen as if they were misbehaving school boys. "You don't quite understand the nature of this movement," she told them. "This movement was inspired and motivated by mothers' love for children.... When they were putting their breakfasts on the table, they saw not only the wheaties and milk, but they also saw Strontium 90 and Iodine 131." (She referred to radioactive elements sometimes present in milk during this time as a result of atomic bomb testing.)

When questioned, the peace strikers spoke passionately as mothers, claiming that protecting their children from nuclear extinction was the essence of "Americanism." What were the congressmen to do

Though properly clad as tidy housewives, women took to the streets to protest the dangers of nuclear testing. Some used their young children as props to demonstrate their stake in the future.

when confronted, literally, with motherhood and apple pie at a time when the virtues of the American home were considered the best antidote to communism? By the end of the third day of the hearings, the chairman of the committee, Clyde Doyle, had completely lost control of the situation. He forbade the spectators to stand. Then he forbade them to applaud. Finally they ran up and kissed the witnesses.

By the time the president of Women Strike for Peace, Dagmar Wilson, was called to the stand and presented with flowers by a young mother in the crowd, the dignified woman demolished the strategy of Doyle and his cronies. When asked if she "would knowingly permit or encourage a Communist party member to occupy a

Dagmar Wilson, president of Women Strike for Peace, presents her demands to a White House policeman. The women called for a stop to the testing of atomic bombs; their signs read, "Stop the Suicide Race."

leadership position in Women Strike for Peace," she coolly replied, "Well, my dear sir, I have absolutely no way of controlling, do not desire to control, who wishes to join the demonstrations and the efforts that women strikers have made for peace. In fact, I would also like to go even further. I would like to say that unless everybody in the whole world joins us in the fight, then God help us."

These women carried the banner of motherhood into politics, a strategy that had been used effectively by their grandmothers in the suffrage movement of the turn of the century. The ability of these women to turn the rhetoric of the Cold War upside down and make a mockery of the dreaded committee hearings signaled that something powerful was beginning to happen among American women. The youth of the 1960s are usually given the credit—or the blame—for the upheavals unleashed during that decade on behalf of civil rights, women's rights, and peace—and for the cultural revolution that shattered the sexual mores and suburban conformity of the 1950s. But it was the parents of that youthful generation—largely their mothers—who paved the way. Women Strike for Peace was one example; the southern civil rights movement, of course, was another.

Some women who lived the typical housewife life during the postwar years became fiery activists later. Betty Goldstein was one such woman. In 1943 she graduated summa cum laude from Smith College and won a graduate fellowship at Berkeley to complete her Ph.D. in psychology. When she told her boyfriend her good news, he let her know that she could choose between him and the fellowship. Crushed and afraid of becoming an "old maid college teacher," she turned down the opportunity, even though the romance did not last.

Goldstein next went to Greenwich Village in New York, rented an apartment with some friends, and went to work as a journalist. But after the war ended and her friends married and moved to the suburbs, she began to fear being left alone. She married Carl Friedan and began having children in the late 1940s. When she was pregnant with her second child, she was fired from her job. For the next several years, Betty Friedan lived the life of a suburban housewife. Yet the education she acquired, her early career as a journalist, and her years of involvement with liberal political causes during the war all set the stage for later activism.

During the dormant '50s, those inclinations were submerged in a sea of domesticity. But in the early '60s, Friedan wrote a book that would capture the attention of educated white women across the country. *The Feminine Mystique* identified the "problem that has no name," the trap of the educated American housewife whose aspirations were stifled within the four walls of the home. Friedan urged her peers to leave their homes, pursue careers, and reject the stifling constraints of postwar domesticity. Her book became an instant best-seller. Women across the country put down Dr. Spock and picked up Betty Friedan. Her book became one of the first statements to pave the way for the new feminist movement that would soon erupt.

By the early '60s, there were signs of dramatic change. President Kennedy established the President's Commission on the Status of Women, chaired by Eleanor Roosevelt, activist first lady from the 1930s. Within the next three years, Congress passed the Equal Pay Act and Title VII of the Civil Rights Act (which prohibited discrimination on the basis of sex, as well as race, color, religion, and national origin), and the United States and the Soviet Union signed the first treaty banning atmospheric testing of nuclear weapons.

While these policies were taking shape, Students for a Democratic Society (SDS), inspired largely by the civil rights movement, gained thousands of members in chapters across the country. This group and others became known as the New Left, because of their call for a radical reorganization of American society. Out of the civil rights and the student movements came the antiwar movement and the new feminist movement. By the late '60s, many hundred thousands of young activists mobilized against the rigid roles for women and men and the devastating sexual mores that had constrained women's lives since the end of World War II.

By the end of the decade, younger women, who emerged with newly discovered skills and strengths from their activism in the civil rights movement and the New Left, organized a new feminist movement. It would move well beyond Betty Friedan's call for self-realization into a full-fledged assault on sexism in all its forms. The new feminists would demand access to professional occupations and skilled jobs, protest low wages, and work for pay equity. They would reject the sexual double standard that had plagued their mothers and would claim their rights to reproductive choice and

Despite her years as a suburban housewife, Betty Friedan never gave up her calling as a journalist. Her book The Feminine Mystique *became the rallying cry of feminism in the early 1960s.*

President John F. Kennedy established the President's Commission on the Status of Women, chaired by former First Lady Eleanor Roosevelt (left). At right is Esther Peterson, whom JFK appointed as director of the Women's Bureau.

legal abortion. These young women were acting on their own behalf, but they had also taken cues from their mothers. As one feisty member of Women Strike for Peace said in 1963, as she called for an end to the bomb-shelter mentality that had prevailed throughout the early Cold War era: "The thought of spending two weeks with two children in a close dark hole [family bomb shelter] was too horrible to think of and we knew we had to do something. Now that we women have started we will no longer be content to be dull uninformed housewives." Women of the 1940s and '50s kept pushing the limits, and eventually they broke through.

CHRONOLOGY

December 7, 1941	Japan attacks Pearl Harbor; U.S. enters World War II
February 19, 1942	President Franklin D. Roosevelt issues Executive Order 9066, authorizing relocation of Japanese Americans from West Coast
1942	Birth Control Federation of America changed to Planned Parenthood Federation of America
1943	Founding of Congress of Racial Equality (CORE)
1944	Founding of National Congress of American Indians (NCAI)
April 12, 1945	President Franklin D. Roosevelt dies; Harry Truman becomes President
August 6-14, 1945	U.S. drops atomic bombs on Hiroshima and Nagasaki; Japan surrenders
1946	Postwar divorces peak before decade-long decline
1946	Equal Rights Amendment (ERA) narrowly defeated in Senate
1947-54	"McCarthy Era": Senator Joseph McCarthy leads anti-Communist crusade
1949	Chinese revolution
1949	William J. Levitt opens first Levittown to suburban families
1950	Televisions enter American homes
1950-53	Korean War
1952	Dwight D. Eisenhower elected President
1954	U.S. Supreme Court rules segregated schools unconstitutional in *Brown* v. *Board of Education*
December 1, 1955	Rosa Parks refuses to give up her seat on a bus to a white passenger; Montgomery, Alabama, bus boycott begins
1957	Peak of the Baby Boom
July 1959	"Kitchen Debate" between Vice President Nixon and Soviet premier Nikita Khrushchev, in Moscow
1960	John F. Kennedy elected President
1960	Food and Drug Administration approves oral contraceptives
November 1, 1961	Women Strike for Peace

FURTHER READING

General Histories

Bernstein, Alison R. *American–Indians and World War II: Toward A New Era in Indian Affairs.* Norman: University of Oklahoma Press, 1991.

Blum, John Morton. *V Was for Victory: Politics and American Culture During World War II.* New York: Harcourt Brace Jovanovich, 1976.

Boyer, Paul. *By the Bomb's Early Light: American Thought and Culture at the Dawn of the Atomic Age.* New York: Pantheon, 1985.

Chafe, William H. *The Unfinished Journey: America Since World War II.* New York: Oxford University Press, 1986.

Daniels, Roger, Sandra C. Taylor, and Harry H. L. Kitano. *Japanese Americans: From Relocation to Redress.* Salt Lake City: University of Utah Press, 1986.

Gilbert, James. *Another Chance: Postwar America, 1945–1985.* 2nd ed. Chicago: Dorsey Press, 1986.

Hall, Jacquelyn Dowd. *Like a Family: The Making of a Southern Cotton Mill World.* Chapel Hill: University of North Carolina Press, 1987.

Hodgson, Godfrey. *America In Our Time: From World War II to Nixon, What Happened and Why.* New York: Random House, 1976.

Jezer, Marty. *The Dark Ages: Life in the United States, 1945–1960.* Boston: South End Press, 1982.

May, Lary, ed. *Recasting America: Culture and Politics in the Age of Cold War.* Chicago: University of Chicago Press, 1989.

O'Neill, William L. *American High: The Years of Confidence, 1945–1960.* New York: Free Press, 1986.

Satterfield, Archie. *The Home Front: An Oral History of the War Years in America, 1941–1945.* New York: Playboy Press, 1981.

Terkel, Studs. *"The Good War": An Oral History of World War II.* New York: Pantheon, 1984.

Histories of Women

Anderson, Karen. *Wartime Women: Sex Roles, Family Relations, and the Status of Women During World War II.* Westport, Conn.: Greenwood Press, 1981.

Chafe, William H. *The American Woman: Her Changing Social, Economic, and Political Roles, 1920–1970.* New York: Oxford University Press, 1972.

_____. *The Paradox of Change: American Women in the Twentieth Century.* New York: Oxford University Press, 1991.

_____. *Women and Equality.* New York: Oxford University Press, 1978.

Cott, Nancy F. *The Grounding of Modern Feminism.* New Haven, Conn.: Yale University Press, 1987.

Cott, Nancy F., and Elizabeth H. Pleck. *A Heritage of Her Own: Toward a New Social History of American Women.* New York: Simon and Schuster, 1979.

DuBois, Ellen Carol, and Vicki L. Ruiz, eds. *Unequal Sisters: A Multi-Cultural Reader in U.S. Women's History.* New York: Routledge, 1990.

Evans, Sara M. *Born for Liberty: A History of Women in America.* New York: Free Press, 1989.

———. *Personal Politics: The Roots of Women's Liberation in the Civil Rights Movement and the New Left.* New York: Knopf, 1979.

Filene, Peter G. *Him/Her/Self: Sex Roles in Modern America.* 2nd ed. Baltimore, Md.: Johns Hopkins University Press, 1986.

Foner, Philip. *Women and the American Labor Movement: From World War I to the Present.* New York: Free Press, 1980.

Franklin, Penelope. *Private Pages: Diaries of American Women, 1830s–1970s.* New York: Ballantine, 1986.

Friedan, Betty. *The Feminine Mystique.* New York: W. W. Norton, 1963.

Gatlin, Rochelle. *American Women Since 1945.* Jackson: University Press of Mississippi, 1987.

Harley, Sharon, and Rosalyn Terborg-Penn. *The Afro-American Woman: Struggles and Images.* Port Washington, N.Y.: Kennikat Press, 1978.

Hartmann, Susan M. *The Home Front and Beyond: American Women in the 1940s.* Boston: Twayne, 1982.

Igus, Toyomi, Veronica Freeman Ellis, Diane Patrick, and Valerie Wilson Wesley. *Great Women in the Struggle: Book of Black Heroes.* Vol. 2. Orange, N.J.: Just Us Books, 1991.

Jones, Jacqueline. *Labor of Love, Labor of Sorrow: Black Women, Work, and the Family from Slavery to the Present.* New York: Basic Books, 1985.

Kaledin, Eugenia. *Mothers and More: American Women in the 1950s.* Boston: Twayne, 1984.

Kennedy, Susan Estabrook. *If All We Did Was to Weep at Home: A History of White Working-Class Women in America.* Bloomington: Indiana University Press, 1979.

Kerber, Linda K., and Jane DeHart Matthews. *Women's America: Refocusing the Past.* New York: Oxford University Press, 1987.

Lamphere, Louise. *From Working Daughters to Working Mothers: Immigrant Women in a New England Industrial Community.* Ithaca, N.Y.: Cornell University Press, 1987.

Lerner, Gerda, ed. *Black Women in White America.* New York: Pantheon, 1972.

Milkman, Ruth. *Gender at Work: The Dynamics of Job Segregation by Sex during World War II.* Urbana: University of Illinois Press, 1987.

Oppenheimer, Valerie Kincade. *The Female Labor Force in the United States.* Westport, Conn.: Greenwood Press, 1970, 1976.

Rosenberg, Rosalind. *Divided Lives: American Women in the Twentieth Century.* New York: Hill and Wang, 1992.

Rothman, Sheila. *Woman's Proper Place: A History of Changing Ideals and Practices, 1870 to the Present.* New York: Basic Books, 1978.

Ruiz, Vicki L. *Cannery Women, Cannery Lives: Mexican Women, Unionization, and the California Food Processing Industry, 1930–1950.* Albuquerque: University of New Mexico Press, 1987.

Rupp, Leila. *Mobilizing Women for War: German and American Propaganda, 1939–1945.* Princeton, N.J.: Princeton University Press, 1978.

Rupp, Leila, and Verta Taylor. *Survival in the Doldrums: The American Women's Rights Movement, 1945 to the 1960s.* New York: Oxford University Press, 1987.

Tsuchida, Nobuya, ed. *Asian and Pacific American Experiences: Women's Perspectives.* Minneapolis: University of Minnesota Press, 1982.

Van Horn, Susan Householder. *Women, Work and Fertility, 1900–1986.* New York: New York University Press, 1988.

Wandersee, Winifred D. *Women's Work and Family Values, 1920–1940.* Cambridge, Mass.: Harvard University Press, 1981.

Family, Reproduction, and Sexuality

Berube, Alan. *Coming Out Under Fire: The History of Gay Men and Women in World War II.* New York: Free Press, 1990.

Brandt, Allan M. *No Magic Bullet: A Social History of Venereal Disease in the United States Since 1880.* New York: Oxford University Press, 1985.

Cherlin, Andrew J. *Marriage, Divorce, Remarriage.* Cambridge, Mass.: Harvard University Press, 1981.

D'Emilio, John. *Sexual Politics, Sexual Communities: The Making of a Homosexual Minority in the United States, 1940–1970.* Chicago: University of Chicago Press, 1983.

D'Emilio, John, and Estelle B. Freedman. *Intimate Matters: A History of Sexuality in America.* New York: Harper & Row, 1988.

Gordon, Linda. *Woman's Body, Woman's Right: Birth Control in America.* New York: Grossman, 1976.

May, Elaine Tyler. *Homeward Bound: American Families in the Cold War Era.* New York: Basic Books, 1988.

Modell, John. *Into One's Own: From Youth to Adulthood in the United States, 1920–1975.* Berkeley: University of California Press, 1989.

Solinger, Rickie. *Wake Up Little Susie: Single Pregnancy and Race before Roe v. Wade.* New York: Routledge, 1992.

Stack, Carol. *All Our Kin: Strategies for Survival in a Black Community.* New York: Harper & Row, 1974.

A Note on Sources

In the interest of readability, the volumes in this series include no discussion of historiography and no footnotes. As works of synthesis and overview, however, they are greatly indebted to the research and writing of other historians. The principal works drawn on in this volume are among the books listed above.

INDEX

Acknowledgments

I would like to thank Nina Morrison, who generously allowed me to use her unpublished senior thesis, "Labors of Love: Women at Work in the Postwar Era, 1947–62," American Studies Progam, Yale University, April 1992. Thanks also to Nancy Toff for her wonderful editorial assistance and to Cynthia Richter for her help with the photos.

Picture Credits

Elaine Tyler May is professor of American studies and history and chair of the American studies program at the University of Minnesota. She is the author of *Homeward Bound: American Families in the Cold War Era*, *Great Expectations: Marriage and Divorce in Post-Victorian America*, and the forthcoming *Barren in the Promised Land: Childless Americans and the Politics of Procreation*. She served on the national council of the American Studies Association and on various committees of the Organization of American Historians and on review panels for the National Endowment for the Humanities. Professor May was a historical consultant for the textbook *American Adventures* and was on the board of associate editors of *Signs: Journal of Women in Culture and Society*. She has received research fellowships from Harvard University, Radcliffe College, the National Endowment for the Humanities, the Rockefeller Foundation, Princeton University, and the American Council of Learned Societies.

Nancy F. Cott is Stanley Woodward Professor of history and American studies at Yale University. She is the author of *The Bonds of Womanhood: "Woman's Sphere" in New England 1780–1835*; *The Grounding of Modern Feminism*; and *A Woman Making History: Mary Ritter Beard Through Her Letters*, editor of *Root of Bitterness: Documents of the Social History of American Women*, and co-editor of *A Heritage of Her Own: Towards a New Social History of American Women*.